f**P**

SHANNON HENRY

—THE—
DINNER
CLUB

How the Masters of
the Internet Universe
Rode the Rise and Fall
of the Greatest Boom
in History

THE FREE PRESS
New York London Toronto Sydney Singapore

THE FREE PRESS
A Division of Simon & Schuster, Inc.
1230 Avenue of the Americas
New York, NY 10020

For information regarding special discounts for bulk purchases,
please contact Simon & Schuster Special Sales:
1-800-456-6798 or business@simonandschuster.com

DESIGNED BY LISA CHOVNICK

Manufactured in the United States of America

1   3   5   7   9   10   8   6   4   2

Library of Congress Cataloging-in-Publication Data

Henry, Shannon.
The Dinner Club : how the masters of the Internet universe rode the
rise and fall of the greatest boom in history / Shannon Henry.
          p.   cm.
          Includes index.
     1. Chief executive officers—Washington Metropolitan Area.
     2. Internet industry—Washington Metropolitan Area.
     3. High technology industries—Washington Metropolitan Area.
          4. Stocks—Washington Metropolitan Area.
     5. Investments—Washington Metropolitan Area.   I. Title.
               HD38.25.U6 H46 2002
          338.7'6004678'0922753—dc21
                    2002028833

ISBN 978-0-7432-2216-7

For Benjamin

And for my parents, Patrick and Dee Henry

CONTENTS

Cast of Characters   XI

Introduction   1

CHAPTER 1   •   Ritz-Carlton Hotel, Washington, D.C.   15

CHAPTER 2   •   The Beginning   26

CHAPTER 3   •   Morton's, Tysons Corner, Virginia   44

CHAPTER 4   •   The Heyday   54

CHAPTER 5   •   Restaurant Nora, Washington, D.C.   91

CHAPTER 6   •   The Crash   100

CHAPTER 7   •   The Georgetown Club,
                        Washington, D.C.   136

CHAPTER 8   •   MicroTragedy   151

CHAPTER 9   •   The Greenfields' House,
                        Potomac, Maryland   183

CHAPTER 10   •   Exit Strategies   189

CHAPTER 11   •   Citronelle, Washington, D.C.   218

CHAPTER 12   •   The Portfolio   228

CHAPTER 13   •   Teatro Goldoni, Washington, D.C.   240

CHAPTER 14   •   The Election   247

Acknowledgments   271

List of Investments   275

Index   277

" . . . Each generation has something different
at which they are all looking."

—Gertrude Stein

"You can't take it with you."

—Moss Hart

CAST OF CHARACTERS

Marc Andreessen, chairman and co-founder, Loudcloud; co-founder, Netscape Communications Corporation (now part of AOL Time Warner); former chief technology officer, America Online.

Alfred R. Berkeley III, vice chairman, the Nasdaq Stock Market; former managing director, Alex, Brown & Sons; captain in the U.S. Air Force, 1968 to 1972.

John Burton, managing director, Updata Capital, Inc., an investment banking and venture capital firm; former president and CEO, Legent Corp.; co-founder, Business Software Technology (BST), which was acquired by Legent.

Steve Case, chairman, AOL Time Warner; former marketer for Pizza Hut and Procter & Gamble.

John M. Fahey, Jr., president and CEO, National Geographic Society; former chairman and CEO, Time Life Inc. subsidiary of Time Warner; former executive vice president and COO, Time-Life Books.

Raul J. Fernandez, CEO, Dimension Data North America; founder, Proxicom, now part of Dimension Data; partner, Lincoln Holdings, which owns the NHL's Washington Capitals and has interests in the NBA's Washington Wizards, the WNBA's Washington Mystics, MCI Center, US Airways Arena, and Ticketmaster Washington/Baltimore; former legislative assistant to Representative Jack Kemp (R-NY).

William F. Gorog, chairman, InteliData; originator of what is now known as LexisNexis; co-founder, chairman, and CEO, Data Corp.; former executive director to the Council on International Economic Policy, reporting to President Ford; former president, Magazine Publishers of America; West Point graduate.

Gary Greenfield, former president and CEO, MERANT; former CEO, INTERSOLV (now part of MERANT); chairman, Information Technology Association of America; U.S. Naval Academy graduate.

Jeong H. Kim, professor at University of Maryland; former group president, Lucent Technologies Optical Networking Group; founder, chairman, and CEO, Yurie Systems, which he sold to Lucent for $1 billion in 1998; former U.S. Naval officer; emigrated from Korea in 1975.

James V. Kimsey, co-founder and chairman emeritus, America Online; former chairman, AOL Time Warner Foundation; West Point graduate; served as airborne ranger in the U.S. Army during Vietnam, rose to rank of major.

Ted Leonsis, vice chairperson, Advanced Services Group, AOL; founder and CEO, Redgate Communications Corp., now part of AOL; majority owner, Lincoln Holdings, which owns the NHL's Washington Capitals and has interests in the NBA's Washington Wizards, the WNBA's Washington Mystics, MCI Center, US Airways Arena, and Ticketmaster Washington/Baltimore.

Alex Mandl, Principal, ASM Investments; former chairman and CEO, Teligent; former president and chief operating officer, AT&T, where he orchestrated the $11.5 billion acquisition of McCaw Cellular; former chairman and CEO, Sea-Land Services, Inc.

Art Marks, general partner, Valhalla Partners and chairman of Mid-Atlantic Venture Association; general partner, venture capital firm New Enterprise Associates from 1984 to 2001; former president of software products, GE Information Services.

Edward J. Mathias, managing director, venture capital firm The Carlyle Group; former director, T. Rowe Price Associates, Inc.

Jack McDonnell, founder, president, and CEO, Transaction Network Services (TNS); former CEO and president, Digital Radio Network; co-founder, Electronic Funds Transfer Association (EFTA).

Bill Melton, founder, former chairman, and CEO, CyberCash; co-founder, VeriFone; founding investor, Transacton Network Services (TNS).

Mario Morino, chairman, Morino Institute (which created the Netpreneur Program); chairman, Venture Philanthropy Partners; co-founder, software firm Morino Associates, which became Legent Corp. and was acquired by Computer Associates in 1995; special adviser, venture capital firm General Atlantic Partners.

Nigel Morris, co-founder, president, and chief operating officer, Capital One, a bank and credit card financial services company; born in the United Kingdom.

Russ Ramsey, co-founder, Friedman, Billings, Ramsey Group, Inc., an investment banking firm; CEO, Capital Crossover Partners, a combination hedge fund–private equity fund; chairman, Capital Investors.

Michael Saylor, co-founder, chairman, and CEO, MicroStrategy, a data mining company; former venture manager, Du Pont.

John Sidgmore, CEO, WorldCom; chairman, ECI2; former vice chairman, Strategy.com, a now-defunct subsidiary of MicroStrategy; former CEO, UUNet, now part of WorldCom, orchestrated UUNet's $2-billion merger with MFS Communications.

Jonathan Silver, general partner, Core Capital Partners; former managing director and chief operating officer, Tiger Management, a New York hedge fund; Assistant Deputy Secretary of the U.S. Department of Commerce from 1992 to 1994; personal adviser to the Secretary of the Treasury.

Rajendra Singh, co-founder and chairman, telecommunications firm LCC International; chairman, Telcom Ventures, which invests in wireless telecommunications companies; co-founder, Teligent; emigrated from India in 1975.

Cast of Characters

Alan Spoon, managing general partner, venture capital firm Polaris Ventures; former president, *The Washington Post* Co., where he held a wide variety of roles from 1982 to 1999; former partner, the Boston Consulting Group.

Steve Walker, founder and CEO, Steve Walker and Associates, a venture capital firm; founder, helicopter service Capital Rising; former CEO, computer security firm Trusted Information Systems (TIS), which was sold to Network Associates.

Mark R. Warner, governor of Virginia (Democrat, elected 2001); co-founder and managing director, venture capital firm Columbia Capital; co-founder, Nextel and Capital Cellular Corp; former chairman of the Democratic Party in Virginia; former candidate for the U.S. Senate.

FUND MANAGERS

Andrew Sachs, president, Capital Investors II; president, Bethany Partners, a private investing firm; former analyst, Morgan Stanley & Co.; co-founder, KMS Investments, a New York angel fund.

Jeff Tonkel, president, Capital Investors I; managing director, Global Internet Ventures (GIV), an Internet holding company co-founded with Bill Melton and Jeong Kim; founder, Reverse Markets, an Internet services firm.

THE
DINNER
CLUB

INTRODUCTION

A few members of the club are gathered at a hotel bar on a warm fall evening, drinking wine and telling stories. With furtive glances of the kind usually reserved for watching stock prices as they scroll across the bottom of the screen, they look up at a television to check on their candidate.

They have weathered much together over the past decade, in business and friendship. Few are billionaires anymore, but most have emerged from the Internet boom and bust with many millions of dollars and an insatiable desire to chase the next challenge.

Tonight, on election eve, they are at the Richmond Marriott to support Mark Warner's quest to become governor of Virginia. Several of the Capital Investors, whom Warner calls "the boys," have swooped in on private planes to watch the first of their own compete for such an office. The news of victory comes first by a cell phone, seconds before the television anchors had word. They rush out from the bar, leaving tables of food and drink, hurry into the elevator, and travel up to the friends, family, and big-donor suite to clink champagne glasses with the winner and new governor-elect, Mark Warner.

Introduction

This is a great moment. But along the way, it was not all parades and acceptance speeches.

On the verge of the Internet boom, this group of friends, the Capital Investors, began meeting once a month for dinner. They would listen to investing pitches, enjoy fine food, and use their relationships to make the most of the unusual opportunity at hand.

I saw them as a microcosm of the best and the worst of this time, and after writing about the group for *The Washington Post,* I asked to cover their dinners for a year on-the-record. The group had become known as the "Super Angels," because they were *angel* investors, a term used for wealthy individuals who fund companies, and they were the richest and most powerful of these private investors.

It was never easy with these guys. In fact, so many things were going so badly at one point during my reporting for this book that the group booted me out. The market was crashing, the members' investments were faltering, and even some of their own companies were teetering on bankruptcy. There was no good news and simply no reason to let a pesky reporter see them at their worst.

The group had agreed to let me in to a certain number of dinners, but then wanted to reassess my continued on-the-record access. The vote to kick me out came on a rainy night after a particularly delicious dinner at Restaurant Nora.

I was waiting in the main room of the restaurant with an

entrepreneur who had presented his business plan to the group that evening. Toward the end of each dinner, start-up founders looking for money are brought in to pitch company ideas to the group. The Capital Investors then decide, that evening, whether to invest, or not. After dessert was served, we were shuttled out of the private room so the investors could make a decision about us.

The members finally walked out, averting their eyes from me, except one who sheepishly whispered, "Call me tomorrow. I'll explain." A couple of them went over to the entrepreneur and patted their hands on his back in congratulations for scoring the funding.

As I searched for a taxi in what had changed from a drizzle to a downpour, I started to panic. The book I wanted to write, had promised to my publisher, and had taken time off to do, was not one that could depend merely on an outsider's view of this dinner club and their activities. This was to be a book where the reader heard the language of the characters and felt as if he were at the table with the members.

It was an agonizing month for me, but thankfully, a wonderful mixture of vanity, trust, and worry got the better of the members and they promptly voted me back in at the next meeting. I'd seen their mercurial temperaments at work while discussing investments and ideas, so I wasn't particularly surprised about the sudden change of heart, although I was much relieved.

I started working on this book a few months after the famed Internet "crash" in the spring of 2000. I'd been covering technology since 1995, first as the Internet and telecommunications reporter for *Washington Technology,* then as the founding editor of *TechCapital* magazine, and since 1998 as a columnist and staff writer for *The Washington Post.*

As a former banking reporter, I was interested in how technology companies were funded and how money fueled concepts that possibly could lead to life-changing technology. But I was also fascinated with the minds and personalities at the top level of these companies. They created a culture that seeped down throughout their ranks, from planning company cruises to handling layoffs. They had wacky visions and enormous egos. But as crazy as these men can be, they think big.

I decided to write this book because an unusual era was ending, and though it is often difficult to see things clearly while they are happening, I felt that if too much time went by, recollections of what occurred would fade away. And I wanted to show that this technology boom and bust did not occur only in the confines of Silicon Valley.

I briefly considered doing a modern history of the Internet. But, like most reporters, I wanted a story no one else could tell. The Capital Investors would be the story because they were the ultimate inner circle of technology power.

Having come up with an idea for the book, I now had several challenges. First, I had to convince the Capital Investors to let me into their dinners on-the-record. There would be no agreements about off-limits subjects or promises to read the manuscript before publication. In addition, I also requested that they not let any other reporters into the dinners for the time that I was working on the book. Second, I needed the support of the *Post,* and third, of course, a publisher.

Why exactly the Capital Investors allowed me into their world begs the question of why anyone bothers talking to a reporter in the first place. People, in general, are pleased when asked their opinion. It involves pride. But I think many in the group have been so busy living this time that they liked the idea of someone stepping back to analyze and preserve the moment. They are too dizzy now, even, to make sense of what happened.

At the dinners, I sat at the table with the members of the club, ate the same meals, and watched entrepreneurs present their plans in hope of recognition. I briefly considered not sitting at the table, but that would have been more distracting. I like to think my presence didn't alter the dinners in any way, but that is impossible to know. Members say they acted no differently when I was there, and they did seem to forget about me once the evening began.

Outside of the dinners, I interviewed the members, their families, competitors, and numerous acquaintances. Some individual members I interviewed many times. Many were unfailingly cooperative, offering insight and thoughts in person by phone and email. Others begrudgingly went along, wondering what would come of it and what exactly would end up in print.

Like the individual members, these dinners took on moods

of their own. At one particular meeting, it was clear from the beginning that the night was not meant to have the festive, free-wheeling atmosphere of so many other evenings. Two founders of companies in which the group had invested stood before them explaining how they'd burned through all of their investment and needed more to survive. It looked like some of the smartest men in business had bet on a bunch of losers.

But not only were the Capital Investors' investments dying, some of the members' own businesses were struggling to survive and every day their stock prices were sinking lower. Bad news was pelting them like little stones as they sipped their wine and shook their heads. It looked bleak. Was it over?

But really, much of the weeping consisted of crocodile tears. Most of the group, fueled by a mixture of ego and newfound fear that they were not invincible after all, began to plan their new ventures. But it was now obvious that none of them was immune from losing everything.

In the mid-1990s, many of those with the clearest opportunistic vision focused on the Internet as a way to explore new ideas and create personal wealth. In another time, these same people would have targeted a different challenge. In Washington, D.C., a couple dozen multimillionaires, including the founders of America Online, the vice chairman of Nasdaq, and the vice chairman of WorldCom, decided to strengthen their chances by forming a dinner club.

Some things were certain: Meetings would be held monthly

in a posh restaurant, where they would gather to consider start-up investments. Other things were less sure. How would the members help one another and what would they learn from one another? Would they change the next generation through their investments and advice?

All-male, the Capital Investors became a new boys' network. They angered some people because they didn't have women members and because their investments at times seemed haphazard. They were often condescending to entrepreneurs who endured the carnival atmosphere of presenting to the group. "It's like a Friday-night frat house," says Russ Ramsey, chairman of the group.

But it was also a rare place where men with unusual new ideas could challenge one another, with the assumption that they understood a common language. It gave them a refuge from the savage business world. At the dinners, they were among friends and let their guard down to relax. How long this self-selected network will endure is unknown. They will continue to meet as long as the dinners are useful and entertaining, which could be forever, or until tomorrow. As the economy faltered and glory days faded, they relied on one another more than ever—for money, favors, votes, and guidance. They were already reinventing themselves.

Ramsey, reacted to the tech crash by creating a combination of a hedge fund and a private equity fund to invest in ailing companies, often called a "vulture fund."

AOL executive Ted Leonsis and web design company founder Raul Fernandez had become fledgling sports moguls and convinced Michael Jordan to come out of retirement to play for the Washington Wizards. Mario Morino began a "venture" philanthropy fund—designed to treat charity like business—that was praised by the corporate-minded but drew questions from traditional philanthropists. AOL co-founders Steve Case and Jim Kimsey moved beyond the technology arena: Case as an international media executive and Kimsey as a self-styled diplomat, occasionally traveling to Colombia to try to broker peace between the rebels and the government.

But alongside the successes there were failures and bitter disappointments, too, and like any group of people, some individuals would do better than others. Several members struggled to keep their companies afloat. Michael Saylor was shaken after settling a lawsuit filed by the U.S. Securities and Exchange Commission and watching his MicroStrategy stock price drop from $333 a share to merely $1. Saylor called the SEC investigation a "witch hunt." Others saw it as the highest-profile Internet fraud accusation of the era and a pivotal moment in the technology market collapse. The way some of the Capital Investors tried to help Saylor rebuild trust while others left him to fight on his own demonstrated the dynamics of the complex relationships among the members.

John Sidgmore staked his considerable reputation on trying to revive the struggling but still No. 2 telecom company, World-

Com, moving from vice chairman to chief executive officer in spring 2002. But shortly after, the company was felled by a massive accounting scandal. Soon after, WorldCom filed for the largest bankruptcy in U.S. history. The WorldCom saga became a symbol of corporate greed and misdeeds.

In the summer of 2002, the three AOLers of the group, Case, Kimsey, and Leonsis, saw their stock pummeled and a general declaration that the two-and-a-half-year-old merger of AOL and Time Warner, once hailed as genius, was a failure. Former executives of the combined company blamed the problems on the company's Internet arrogance, saying AOL had marched into the deal thinking it had a superior "DNA" to traditional media companies.

"An infectious greed seemed to grip much of our business community," said Federal Reserve Board Chairman Alan Greenspan in July of 2002, attempting to explain the excesses of the late 1990s.

As the members were having these adventures, a new ideology was formed during the late 1990s and early 2000s. It was a different way of thinking represented by people who were richer, younger, and more idealistic than those who amassed wealth in the 1980s. They don't just want to leave their money to heirs, but instead they crave the instant gratification of seeing it spent in ways that might change something, now. These people are important to know because their cash and power will be felt well beyond their own children and the beneficiaries of their foundations.

There is friction, however, between the tech elite and those who dislike them because they're rich and accustomed to getting their way. As they move into new realms, the Capital Investors are challenged by people who say that although they may know technology and finance, they have little grounding in media, sports, philanthropy, and politics. And they do have to live down some of the craziness.

But those who flourished in this Internet age of course lapped up the attention and reveled in over-the-top performances. The front of one invitation in September of 1998 read *Celebrate the Great Gatsby!*

"It was an age of miracles, it was an age of art, it was an age of excess, it was an age of satire," it declared. It was also the sixtieth birthday party of AOL co-founder Jim Kimsey, a man flush with Internet cash. The Roaring Twenties seemed back again, if only for a moment.

The party was held at F. Scott's, a bar in Georgetown, and the AOL-ers and other guests wore boas and flapper dresses, zoot suits and wide-brimmed fedoras. Kimsey introduced himself as Gatsby that evening and his financial adviser and girlfriend at the time, Holidae Hayes, as Daisy. It was pretend, but strangely real. Actually, Kimsey probably has more money than Gatsby could ever imagine.

A penchant for the '20's era was common among other Internet millionaires and the members of the club who naturally related to Gatsby's brief but intense sunny moment. Software entrepreneur and philanthropist Mario Morino held his 2000 annual Christmas party for 200 friends with the theme of '20's gangsters and rumrunners. But by then it was the end of an era, with some of the members' companies filing for bankruptcy and others moving on to loftier ambitions.

Some of them recognized the ridiculousness of it all and didn't hesitate to mock themselves and their time. Surely, if Gatsby had existed in the late 1990s, he would have been an angel investor or venture capitalist.

As individuals, the Capital Investors are twenty-six very different people. Several have enough greed for the whole table; others are confident but modest. "Each of us has our own drummer we listen to," says Bill Gorog, the oldest member of the group, who was one of the inventors of the LexisNexis system. But there are several things most of them have in common. They are not trust-fund wealthy, and many of them grew up poor and are self-made. Many of them were told at some point that they couldn't accomplish a particular goal, and they have a passion to prove that naysayer wrong. They had an interest in technology before most people saw its true promise. They want to change the world in some way, which, depending on how you look at it, is admirable or frightening. Another common trait is a restless idealism that sends them perpetually in search of something, especially after they have achieved the last mission. This impatience, especially for the younger members of the group, is physical. It manifests itself in tapping feet, the tendency to rearrange silverware, the simple inability to sit still. Group member and venture capitalist Art Marks calls it "achievement disease." "If you're not achieving, you're not breathing," he says. "No one in the group can rest."

The Capital Investors can be bratty and unpredictable in these meetings. At one dinner, Steve Case asked a presenter whether his technology made it easier to telemarket during supper time. When the answer was yes, Case threw a roll at the entrepreneur. But the members can also quickly understand an entrepreneur's technology, give sage advice, and when the mood strikes them, genuine encouragement. Many of them do seem to remember that it was not so long ago they were in that newcomer's place.

"One on one they are fairly benevolent," says Esther Smith, who co-founded business newspaper *Washington Technology* and has been friends with several of the members for years. "But as a group they can be destructive. I've advised companies not to go to them." Smith, who now advises start-up companies, says that's because if the entrepreneur is turned down, his reputation could be marred by the rejection.

What turned out to be the real downfall, of course, was that many of the companies created during the Internet frenzy simply didn't have profits or customers. Much of it turned out to be a lonely and dreary fairy tale. The story wasn't true. "They were Hollywood façades," says Washington venture capitalist Jack Biddle about some of the biggest-buzz technology companies.

Not all of them were fakes, however. New ways of communicating and doing business evolved during the era. And the members of the Capital Investors were bigger players than the tiny dot-coms.

There is something oddly familiar about the rise and fall of technology in Washington, a city where people's fortunes and reputations are often decimated by a single act or a prevailing vote. "Everything in this town is a trend, whether it's the four-year term or health care," says Raul Fernandez, a former Capitol Hill staffer who founded and sold a Web design company, watched his wealth go from $1.1 billion to $211 million, and became partners with Michael Jordan.

"It was a once-in-a-lifetime convergence of events," he says.

It was also an age of entitlement, where not only the Capital Investors, but start-up entrepreneurs and everyday investors thought if they didn't become rich during this time, something was wrong with them.

Many of the members of the Capital Investors are what anthropologist Michael Maccoby calls "productive narcissists," creatures of an economic boom and the fast-paced technological innovation that came along with those times. "They've always done things that others say can't be done," says Maccoby. "The fact that this country produces people like that has pros and cons. You could get into trouble or you could do great things. There's something both wonderful and incredibly naïve about these people."

Great opportunities at unsual moments in time draw obsessive, driven people like these who rose and fell in the first generation of the Internet era. Marc Andreessen looks at it this way:
Better they are capitalists than dictators. "They could be out
raising armies and starting religions" instead, he says. "You don't
want these people loose on the streets. Building a company
allows you to optimize your personal gain and affect social
good. It's the only place they are socially useful."

Now, this new club is changing the economy and culture in
a way that they hope will leave a legacy bigger than a monu-
mental bank account. In fact, merely making more money has
lost appeal.

Raj Singh, an immigrant from India who grew up without
running water or a telephone, has a net worth that has fallen
from billionaire level to that of a mere multimillionaire—from
$4 billion to about $500 million, by his estimate. He feels he has
helped transform the American economy.

"You make $100 million and you feel very excited about it.
But then you make the next $200 million and it's nothing," says
Singh. "It makes you want to do something else."

Only certain types of people are willing to risk everything.
These tycoons, at once brilliant and boorish, shaped this era as
much as it molded them. They developed an addiction to the
speed and impact of technological change. And now, they are
not content to stand still. They are armed with the money and
influence of a time that for this generation may not come again.

CHAPTER ONE

RITZ-CARLTON HOTEL, WASHINGTON, D.C.

November 2000

J IM KIMSEY SWAGGERS INTO the private room at the Ritz-Carlton, opens his wallet, and pulls out a business card.

Gathered for cocktails before the seven o'clock dinner, Bill Melton, Mario Morino, and Russ Ramsey circle Kimsey, peering over his shoulder in the red-wallpapered Jefferson Room. The card reads *Fidel Castro*. Everyone laughs. It just seems as though Castro shouldn't need a business card. Kimsey shows this memento as a lead-in to tell the group that he's just back from a trip to Cuba where he visited the aging dictator. The men had a seven-hour dinner together where they talked about the Internet, Castro's health, and politics. Kimsey, who co-founded America Online, has been on a different kind of mission lately, traveling around the world preaching capitalism to international leaders, especially those currently practicing socialism and Marxism. Cuba's his latest call, but he's been to meet rebel commanders in Colombia and the president of Indonesia, too. Kimsey says that since stepping down as the chairman of AOL, he has become a kind of accidental ambassador, a Forrest Gump of diplomacy. But Kimsey, who favors French-cuffed shirts and travels around Washington by limousine, is more focused on this work than he admits. He is quite self-aware as he embarks on each mission of influence, armed with American charisma and cash.

Kimsey proudly announces that after five and a half hours of drinking *mojitos,* martinis, and fine wine, it was Castro who had to get up to go to the bathroom first.

In two days, Kimsey will go to Vietnam with President Clinton. This upcoming trip, especially because Kimsey fought in Vietnam, is considered by his friends to be an honor, a sign that Kimsey is beginning to be recognized as he wants to be: as an international statesman (skip the elder part, he'd say). The visit to the guerrilla camps in Colombia, however, worried some of the members who know kidnapping is big business there; it makes them wonder what exactly the government wants from their friend. They think he is crazy for going. He says he's just on an adventure.

As the waiter takes drink orders and delivers them on a silver tray, talk turns to sports and vacations. Not to be outdone in showmanship, investment banker Ramsey talks about a recent triathlon he completed and Rajendra Singh, a telecom investor and one of the wealthiest in the group, wearing a bright red sweater, talks about a marathon. Melton is just back from Paris, where he and his playwright wife have a home and are trying to spend a quarter of their time.

The group usually doesn't invite outsiders, and even their wives aren't allowed in. But tonight they have a guest speaker for the evening, former Republican Party chairman Haley Barbour, here in the midst of the 2000 presidential voting process, to explain the election that never seemed to end. Barbour listens to their stories as he sips his cocktail. He has an expression on his face that asks, "Are these people for real?"

While they're usually more casually dressed at the dinners, tonight several are in suits and red ties, perhaps in honor of the political guest. The men sit down at a long table, set with the Ritz's trademark cobalt blue glasses. The wine is poured, a 1998 Sancerre Pascal Jolivet and a 1997 Ferrari-Carano Merlot. As soon as they are seated, several of the Capital Investors pull out their BlackBerrys, handheld devices that have become appendages to the high-tech. Using their thumbs, they check and send email, glancing up occasionally to make sure they aren't missing anything. They are here, but not really here.

But as the conversation begins, they shove the devices aside and fall into that rare world they look forward to each month, where they are among people they consider friends and equals.

The presidential election, to most in the group, has been a horrible embarrassment. The chad jokes start. "It used to be a Third World country," says Kimsey.

These businessmen are used to accountability through stock price and success measured in quarters. Most of them are still on a high from the straight-up prosperity of the past few years, as they made it big in the electronic gold rush either through their own technology companies or by high-tech investing, often in one another's businesses. The message is clear: If they were in charge of the country, this election mess never would have happened.

As dinner is served on yellow and gold china, starting with agnolotti with porcini mushrooms, a debate heats up about the legal aspects of the election, leading into questioning about what exactly should be done.

Venture capitalist Alan Spoon talks about the inefficiencies of counting the results, measured in "ballots per minute."

"What are the options?" demands Michael Saylor of the group, as if he is gathering enough information to decide exactly what should be done for the country right here, right now.

Saylor emits several agitated sighs and twirls his fork in a circle before answering his own question in a high-pitched monotone. "It will probably go to the Supreme Court," says Saylor, who is chief executive of data mining firm MicroStrategy. "It's a statistical deadlock," Saylor continues. "They both ought to walk away." He says that if a statistician were analyzing the results, he would suggest they both throw in the towel and pick someone else to be president.

Telecom investor Singh is starting to get annoyed, too. He wants to solve this problem. He became a billionaire several times over after arriving in the United States in 1975 from a tiny town in India with no money to his name. He went blind in one eye as a child when a stray arrow hit him in the face.

"All this nonsense is theoretical. What can this group do that is constructive?" Singh asks.

There is more BlackBerrying going on, more shifting in seats.

"So what can people do, particularly people with some wealth?" demands Singh.

Barbour gets his "I'm on an alien planet" look again.

"One thing this group can do is try to understand how technology can be used in a federal system," says Kimsey. "To be using 1950's technology is silly."

"It's embarrassing," adds Saylor.

They don't take shame lightly.

"We've gotten lots of feedback from Castro and China and people saying 'You want us to follow your model? Hee hee hee.' They're having a high old time," says Kimsey.

"We could underwrite a process where Michael Saylor can study this process," he suggests dryly.

"I think it's a massive crisis of competence in the system," pronounces Saylor. "We are playing dice with the election."

Spoon comments that the process opened a can of maggots no one expected to see and Melton talks about the "bell curve" of campaigns.

Amongst the chatter, Mario Morino makes a small noise as if he wants to say something.

"Let Mario talk," says Ramsey.

"When half your population doesn't vote, technology doesn't do a god-damn thing," Morino says. "This is about people. This is not about technology."

Morino calls it the "impulse election."

Saylor suggests using the Internet to let people register the day of the vote. No one would pay taxes weeks ahead of when he actually had to pay them, so why do people have to register so far ahead of the vote?

"You trust that stuff but the rest of the population doesn't," says Melton. "You're preaching to the choir."

Morino says speeding up the process could be a mistake. "You can't expect democracy to be perfect, only fair," says Singh.

Singh, anxious again, proposes the group put $40 million in the bank to create a fund that would improve the election process. He says Karl Marx taught that the richest lost the most in troubled times, and Singh thinks the economy is about to get a lot worse.

"We have the most to lose, guys. If the economy goes down, who has the most to lose? The people in this room," he says.

"How would we do this?" Singh asks Barbour.

There are laughs and fleeting looks around. Everyone

understands Singh is completely serious, but no one jumps in with an offer of how much he'd put into an election-process-overhaul fund.

Saylor, who has a bad cold tonight, again starts complaining about the untrained workers who run the election system.

"He's not going to solve voting tonight," says Ramsey.

The debate rages on as the entrepreneurs scheduled to present tonight wait outside. Andrew Sachs, who manages the Capital Investors fund, motions to Ramsey that it's time to start the pitches. Ramsey looks annoyed. This conversation is fun, and he doesn't want to interrupt it.

"Can we just tell the entrepreneur we'll invest?" Ramsey says.

Sachs smiles slightly and goes out to stall.

Jonathan Silver, a venture capitalist and former economic aide to the Clinton administration, wonders out loud what Governor George W. Bush would accomplish should he win.

The group moves on to a discussion about other candidates. Will Hillary Rodham Clinton run in four years? And then they begin to talk about one of them—a technology magnate—running the country sometime in the next decade.

"Bill Gates will be bored by then," says Saylor. Larry Ellison . . . or what about Michael Dell? Does he have any political aspirations?"

Up until now, political Washington and technology Washington haven't mixed much, although they are influencing each other in many ways. Several members of the group have a "chief of staff" who is in charge of the CEO personally—from business deals to charities to press. And Saylor's thirty-fifth birthday invitation to a party at trendy restaurant Cities in Adams Morgan announced that they would be celebrating his reaching the legal age to run for the presidency. The first of their group to actually run for office, Mark Warner, lost a Senate race to John Warner in 1996. But Mark is preparing to run again, for governor of Virginia in 2001. His friends are supporting him, with most of the Capital Investors as his top donors. If Warner wins, he'll take his own influence—and those who helped him along—to a higher level than control over a company or two.

At the Ritz-Carlton tonight, as the racks of lamb and Chilean sea bass are being polished off, these political discussions seem much more important than an entrepreneur's presentation. But the group is an investment club after all, and the executives of Network Mantra have been waiting in the lobby outside now, unfed, for two hours. Finally, two Indian entrepreneurs dressed in suits come in. The Capital Investors start flipping through their ten-page handout describing the company's plan. Suprotik Ghose speaks in a calm, even tone, peppering his presentation with tech-terms like *functionality, key differentiators,* and *vendor agnostic.* He has created software that makes it easier to manage a computer network. He lists Cisco as a key competitor, as well as other start-ups called Goldwire and ISP Soft. This market he's going after, he says, is worth $13 billion.

Everyone is quiet, picking at chocolate nut tarts. Really, they'd still rather be talking about how to change the political system.

Finally Ramsey asks, as if to merely break the silence, which companies Network Mantra has chosen to test the software on first. "Who are your beta customers?"

There is more talk about *webification, enterprise networks,* and *e-commerce revolution.*

"Who is the strongest guy on your team in sales and marketing?" asks Melton.

"That's an excellent question, sir," replies Ghose, who answers by saying the company is now looking to hire sales people.

"On your management team, you have a lot of Indians, do you need some extra chiefs?" jokes Singh.

"You're the only one who could say that," says Kimsey.

"I've lived what you're going through in another generation," offers Morino. Ghose says ideally, they'd like to sell their company to Cisco. "It's a company everyone wants to sell their company to," says Ghose.

Saylor, who has his initials "MJS" monogrammed on his shirt cuffs, is checking his BlackBerry and sighing.

"We want to build customer traction by using our contacts," says Suri Bulusu. "And maybe your contacts."

Sachs ends the presentation by saying thanks. Everyone claps.

The entrepreneurs are shuttled out and Atlantic McClellan,

a tall, pretty young woman who looks after the logistics of the dinners, such as the restaurant and wine choices, goes out to keep them company.

The group now decides whether to invest or not, which is usually a highly arbitrary discussion. Sometimes they vote. Sometimes they don't. Sachs says Network Mantra is talking to Teligent about doing a deal, so it's too bad Teligent chief executive Alex Mandl isn't here to weigh in.

"They're not building a company, they're building a technology," says Kimsey. "They're building this for a quick buck. They are totally on flip mode."

"They're not as far ahead in the O-S-S world as they say they are," says Spoon.

"There is a market. The question is who's going to make the most sales," says Melton.

"The co-founder's body language was horrible," says Ramsey. "Did you see him?"

"I think we probably have better things we can invest in," says Saylor. "I can say nothing more persuasive than that."

The group starts to talk about what not investing will mean to the company. Will it be bad for its reputation? Is there someone else they should introduce to the executives?

"We could do them a favor by sending them to another company," says Spoon.

"You always bet on the management team. They should be a sub-team in another company," says Melton.

Saylor is clearly fed up with the discussion, and especially with the niceties of saying no. "Are we kind of wasting time here?" he asks. "We're not excited by these guys. Even if you flip a company, you have to act like you aren't going to flip."

"You know what you get when you cross a lemming with a sheep? A venture capitalist," says Kimsey, laughing.

"I'm going to hit the rest room," says Singh. "You can talk about Indians all you want."

And it's over.

"They should know we have no ax to grind, no careers to save," says Kimsey. "We don't give a shit." Sachs is told to "synthesize" this feeling to the entrepreneurs, who are waiting in the lobby again, expecting a yes or no. The Capital Investors take last sips of their wine or coffee and disperse into the autumn night to their cars or limos, having not quite solved the problems of the world. But there's always next month.

CHAPTER TWO

THE BEGINNING

I T I S C H A R A C T E R I S T I C of the Capital Investors that the members can't agree on where exactly the idea for the invitation-only dinner and investing club first was hatched. One person remembers a gathering at the Hidden Creek Country Club in Reston, Virginia, in 1996, just after the federal government opened the Internet to commercial enterprise. Another thinks a meeting at the Four Seasons in Georgetown was key, and someone else tells the story of a pow-wow at Italian eatery Maggiano's in Tysons Corner.

The twenty-six members also have twenty-six different ideas about how things should be done and each is used to getting his way. "It's like herding cats," says Andrew Sachs, twenty-seven, who manages the group's investment fund and who many of the members call "the kid."

Wherever that first meeting was, the group, led by investment banker Russ Ramsey, software engineer and philanthropist Mario Morino, and telecom investor Mark Warner, began regularly convening in Washington in 1997 just before the height of Internet frenzy. With shared goals and interests, and a common worry that they could miss something big, they were drawn together to seize a moment.

"Capital markets are driven by fear and greed," says Ramsey.

Many of the original members had never met one another before. Some, like Steve Walker and Jack McDonnell, were former Defense Department technologists who had worked at the Internet's birthplace, the Defense Advanced Research Projects Agency (DARPA) at the Department of Defense; others, like Art Marks and Jonathan Silver, were money men, investors in dozens of companies who sit on a half dozen or so boards. But they all sensed an unusual opportunity was arising, and they were looking to find others who would understand their talk and help them make the most of what would be a short burst of wealth-making and entrepreneurial chance. In the meantime, they would attempt to re-create a political town as a technology capital by encouraging entrepreneurship, new investment funds, and personal networking. If it worked, they would build a community from the ground up and become rich in the process.

Being a Washington club makes for a different personality than that of angel clubs in Silicon Valley or other technology hot spots. People have always come to Washington in their young careers to change the world. By contrast, says Andreessen, people come to the Valley with the sole goal of starting companies. If they want to do something else, they go somewhere else.

"In Washington, the proximity to the political and economic

heartbeat of the world molds the entrepreneur in a different way," says investment banker George Stamas, who has done many deals with the Capital Investors.

Many of the group serve as a shadow cabinet to U.S. and world leaders, especially in areas of technology and finance. Jeong Kim is a member of an eight-person presidential task force on U.S. intelligence issues. And Kim and Alex Mandl serve on the board of In-Q-Tel, a venture capital fund run by the Central Intelligence Agency. Yes, even the CIA wanted in on the tech boom.

Washington also shapes relationships in a different way. The Capital Investors are tied by what are very much Washington friendships, a hybrid of work and play relationships. This kind of friendship makes it more difficult to find true friends. "In challenging, dark times and really good times, the phone and email are really silent," says Ramsey. "I've had spectacularly good things happen to me when I didn't get a single call." But it makes people more likely to keep real friends close when they do find them.

"These are the people who would be the catalysts," says Morino of the members of the group. "We asked, 'Who would you want to have dinner with to create a force?'" The group could not wait for people who didn't understand how the Internet was about to change things. "There was no time," Morino says. Assemble the strongest people who "get it" in a room and let them form an even stronger power together, they thought.

"In this Petri dish we had all the germs floating around, they just needed to be connected," says Morino.

The group formed as Washington business executives were trying to establish their place in the technology revolution. Even with top companies in telecom, Internet services and Web content all in the region, they had Silicon Valley envy. Business people in Washington, unless they had political connections or were one of a few old-Washington family-owned companies, rarely felt part of the inner circle of the town. "This region had an identity crisis," says Russ Ramsey. "How do we fit? How do we get respect?" There was angst that Washington did not have a Silicon Valley–type moniker, which was followed by a series of ill-fated naming attempts. The Capital Investors did not name the region, but they gave it a personality.

"We didn't have role models," says venture capitalist Ed Mathias of Washington's business community before the Internet era.

Jeff Tonkel managed the fund before Sachs and now runs a $140-million international fund for two of the members, CyberCash founder Bill Melton and Jeong Kim, who founded a telecom networking company Kim sold to Lucent. Tonkel sat down one day to draw a map of the groups' connections, trying to measure how valuable his new contacts were. He figures you can get to any CEO in the country within one to three phone calls from members of the club. It's the Capital Investors' three degrees of separation. Many are on particularly strategic boards that range from computers to clothing: Alex Mandl sits on Dell's board; Spoon is a director of Human Genome Sciences; Warner and Fernandez serve on the boards of George Washington University and Liz Claiborne, respectively.

Sachs signed on as fund managers of the group after Mark Warner discovered him running an angel fund for Sachs's cousin, a producer of the Broadway musical *Rent*.

From the beginning, the social network was the reason most kept coming back every month. After a day of people asking them for things, not giving their real opinions to the boss, and angling for something, they look forward to meeting with their peers. As much as they talk over one another in louder and louder voices and often disagree, there is a basic sense that everyone is on the same level. And they have fun. As the wine flows, the jokes start; no one takes anyone else too seriously. Socials, where wives are invited, are held once or twice a year at members' homes.

But these are calculated friendships. Many have genuine affection for one another, but group members are using these relationships to get ahead faster and help one another succeed. Many of the members put up their money and contacts to help Morino create a $35-million "venture" philanthropy fund, which has a more businesslike way of charitable giving than traditional nonprofits. After the technology market crash of 2000, Ramsey, with a little help from his friends, raised a $200-million combination hedge fund–private equity fund to invest in troubled companies, which suddenly were bargains. And when Michael Saylor's stock was falling, his company, MicroStrategy, was being investigated by the SEC for fraud, and his personal image tarnished in the press, some—but not all—of the Capital Investors rallied around him, with then WorldCom vice chairman John Sidgmore even agreeing to run a division of Micro-Strategy. They aid one another, too, with behind-the-scenes introductions, advice, and subtle pushes that keep the members moving in the right direction.

"I can call people for them who they may not want to call, like someone who would buy them, or invest in them, or join their board," says Al Berkeley, vice chairman of Nasdaq. "Those guys are friends. Friends have immediate access," he says. "I would put special effort in for any of those guys." He says he's watching out for his friends from his vantage point on the market, a perk many outside the club would like to have.

Berkeley, like several of the other Capital Investors, has a daredevil, offbeat sense of humor. For many years, one of the greatest mysteries of the Washington area was who had placed a 250-pound Black Angus cow on top of the University of Virginia rotunda in 1965 (not to mention how the person got the cow up there). Finally, in the late 1990s at a UVA alumni event, Berkeley owned up to the college prank, which had unfortunately led to the death of the cow.

Each has gone through complex financial, emotional, and logistical issues that all company leaders must face. "You have experience in going through the same set of successes or failures that, when somebody says something, you know what he's talking about because you have seen it somewhere in your own life," says Singh.

And, Singh says, while he understands it's difficult for normal people to muster much sympathy for the superrich, things really can be unbearably lonely at the top. "Many of the people in this kind of group are very isolated people. They don't have too many people to talk to, they don't have too many outlets. I believe that they always have a problem because whenever someone is talking to them, they have an agenda."

Still, as much as they help one another, they are also, naturally, fiercely competitive. Holidae Hayes, an investment banker who manages the personal investments of about a half-dozen of the members and is a former girlfriend of Kimsey's, says they are always asking her about the others' net worth.

"They are little boys on the playground at recess," she says. Even after achieving success, they feel they still have much to prove.

These barons of the Beltway are far from old money. Mostly in their forties, the Capital Investors didn't have famous parents or family riches. One grew up in a mobile home, several are immigrants who came to Washington with a few dollars in their pockets. For many of them, wealth has happened quickly and surprisingly. It was not so long ago they were on the outside of the group looking in.

One thing that makes this generation of barons different from that of the Fords or Rockefellers was that their fortunes could—and did—rise or fall in an instant. It gives them a different sense of timing. While it would take decades to build, say, an oil or railroad empire, these men hit their peak at a wonderful, strange moment when anything could happen, no matter who you were.

Kids have secret tree house clubs, then fraternities or sororities, then usually less-formal groups, or sometimes salons. There's a password to get in, a list of (sometimes unspoken) rules, and a powerful camaraderie that rewards favors and punishes betrayal. They are a safe haven for the accepted and a reminder of the unfairness of life for those who are shut out. This is a grown-up boys' club where the members have the money and power to alter the course of business.

The Capital Investors group was built as an opposite to the 123 Club, a secretive society of Washington business leaders formed during the golden age of real estate, the early 1980s, and named for Route 123 where the highest commercial rents were demanded.

While the 123 Club was old in age and style, Capital Investors would be cutting-edge, young, with few neckties in the room. Warner remembers being in a 123 Club meeting, looking around and realizing he was at least twenty years younger than everyone else in the room. "I thought it would be cool to have a group of the next generation," he says.

Still, defining the Capital Investors' mission is a constant struggle between those who simply like the fraternity aspect and those who think the group must also have a higher purpose, like investing in start-ups and giving them advice. Some in the group think they should invest in a good idea with a leader they want to support, others don't want to bet on anything that won't win. This conflict has resulted in an eclectic portfolio of impulse investments.

"Guys can't get together without an ulterior motive," explains member Jonathan Silver, a venture capitalist and former economic adviser to President Clinton. "It's like golf. You know why guys play golf? Guys play golf because it legitimizes their excuse to take a lovely walk in the park. No guy can say, 'I'm going to take a lovely walk in the park.' And the same thing holds true here. We're going to invest in companies because we have to have a reason, we can't get together purely for fellowship because what man would do that?" So the official raison d'être became smallish ($100,000 to $300,000) investments in young companies.

While at first a Capital Investor nod would help a company get in to see venture capitalists and aid in other connections, as the group became more focused on their own companies, and as seed capital became easier to find, their stamp of approval became less important.

As the group evolved, new members were nominated and voted on at meetings, always keeping the number around twenty-five. Two have quit: venture capitalist David Gladstone and telecommunications executive Daniel Akerson. According to group members, Gladstone disagreed with the club's evolving mission, and Akerson became irritated by Michael Saylor's speeches. No woman has ever been invited into the club. The members defend that decision by saying she would only be a figurehead, and that there is really no woman in Washington business quite up to the membership requirements. One African-American was asked to join, Robert Johnson, chairman of Black Entertainment Television, but he turned the group down. Johnson says he prefers to make personal investments on his own rather than as part of a group.

Several members originally hail from other countries: Mandl is from Austria, Morris from the United Kingdom. Kim emigrated from Korea to the Washington suburbs with his family in 1975 when he was fourteen, putting himself through school working in a 7-Eleven before joining the U.S. Navy. Singh came to America the same year to study engineering and never moved back to the tiny village in India where he grew up.

The Capital Investors say there's no net worth cutoff; membership is offered because the others in the group simply want to get to know that person better. When Marc Andreessen, creator of Netscape and now chairman of Loudcloud, moved to Washington after AOL bought Netscape, he joined the Capital Investors to get an instant introduction to the top Washington players. He has since moved back to Palo Alto, but is still a member, though he hasn't been to a meeting in a long time. Alan Spoon, too, is now an out-of-town member. Spoon was for years the CEO of *The Washington Post* Co. Wanting to get closer to the tech boom, he joined Polaris, a venture capital firm in Boston. "I felt I needed to get into the new economy," explained Spoon. Over the years, Case has shown up to fewer and fewer dinners, although he does pop in every now and then, goes to some of the social events, and keeps re-investing in the fund.

Warner says these are carefully chosen friends for people who don't have time for friends. "Some people would meet the criteria in terms of business leadership and success, but didn't meet the criteria of wanting to have dinner with them once a month," says Warner. If one member doesn't like a candidate, he can strike a name off the list, provided that member happens to be around when the discussion takes place.

"You can't get into the group unless you know someone in the group," adds John Burton. In the Internet age as in all others, there are clubs who will keep out whom they don't want.

Strengthening the network is a multi-tiered interconnection: whether it's doing deals together, sharing board seats, or having their kids in the same school. Raj Singh was on the board of Teligent, when Alex Mandl was the company's CEO. CyberCash founder Bill Melton joined AOL's board at Jim Kimsey's request, having met Kimsey through venture capitalist Frank Caufield, who was on the AOL board and Melton's board at VeriFone. Singh is a limited partner in Silver's Core Capital venture fund.

Gorog provided initial financing to VeriFone, and Melton was a founding funder of McDonnell's Transaction Network Services. Leonsis and Morino served on Fernandez's Proxicom board.

During the early years of the Capital Investor meetings, the number of technology workers threatened to eclipse the number of government employees in Washington. It became hotter to work for a start-up than on Capitol Hill. In 1999, three of the youngest members—Raul Fernandez, Michael Saylor, and Jeong Kim—were listed on *Fortune* magazine's roster of the forty richest Americans under the age of forty. And those who made all this money began to show up in the social pages of newspapers and among the buyers of the largest homes, Washington's new rich.

As the group met, their counterparts in other areas of the country were also trying to figure out how to transform their area into a tech capital, to cash in on the moment. And it turned out that despite the Internet being everywhere, certain geographies became more successful than others. They all wanted to be the "other" Silicon Valley, and they all had wanna-be names, like Silicon Alley in New York, or Digital Coast in Los Angeles. Every few months, someone new to Washington would champion a name for the region: the Netplex, Mid-Atlantech, Beltway Bandwidth, Silicon Dominion, Techtopia. None caught on.

"When you try to market yourself, most people ignore you," says Morino, who points out that most of the region's naming attempts seemed desperate.

"Angel" networks also flourished in this time, but most had

hundreds of members. Exclusive investing groups like the Capital Investors are rare. An all-women angel investing club sprouted up in Washington, in part a reaction to the tendency of Capital Investors and other angel clubs to not invite women. Patty Abramson, one of the founders of WomenAngels.net, knows many of the Capital Investors. She calls the group a "good ol' boys' network."

Silver says there are many deals the group has done that his own investing firm, Core Capital Partners, wouldn't have touched. Still, he says, the members are not in the club to make money. That's good, because the portfolio, like that of many venture capital firms, is certainly struggling. "You're betting relatively small chips on a number of spaces, to use the roulette analogy," says Mandl. "The odds are that some of those, a relatively small percentage, will do very well." That was the idea, of course. But as technology business sank in the early 2000s, that thought began to seem outdated and overly optimistic.

When the Capital Investors formed, there was little "seed capital" for a start-up in Washington that didn't come from any of the three F's—friends, family, and fools. That first big-break money, one or two blockbuster technology companies, availability of later-stage venture capital, and proximity to research-based colleges and universities were considered the necessary ingredients for a successful technology region.

They weren't going to create a Stanford from scratch, and they did think, like Silver says, that they needed a serious reason to meet. So the Capital Investors decided that the most valuable thing they could provide was this early-stage money, plus some of their been-there advice. So each member put up a small sum, which, depending on how long they have been in the group, is between $100,000 and $300,000. And they invited start-ups to present their ideas during the dinners, which are held in the private rooms of the best restaurants in Washington. The group would then decide—that night, often while the presenter waited outside—if it would invest in the company. The Capital Investors hoped to say by example that the community needs re-investment, and that this little portion of their net worth, money that could have gone to an out-of-town company or into the stock market, would go right back to their roots.

And the members of the group would get a first look at companies that might be their own competitors. It could be a first big break for a little company, or a bit of inside intelligence for the Capital Investors.

"It's like being a grandfather," says Steve Walker about angel investing. "We get to offer advice but then we don't have to make all the details happen."

However, there was a glitch in the investment process. Capital Investors has a rule that they don't do "follow-on" investments, meaning a company gets a chunk of money once and that's it. The Capital Investors won't come in later to save the day, although individual members could choose to re-invest.

This is a particular problem for CI portfolio companies because one of the ways potential new investors gauge the success of a company is how interested current investors are in coming back in. It's an obvious sign of approval for an investor to keep pouring their money in a company. "They have one hand tied behind their back," says angel investing expert John May about the Capital Investors.

The members clearly don't care much if they make any money from the investments. They joke that their investments in these companies are "rounding errors." But as much as they belittle some of the companies that present to them, they would love to spot a new technology or fledgling star executive at an early moment.

"I think *they* still think they'll discover the next Microsoft," says Cal Simmons, who with May runs several angel clubs. "We're less likely to find the next Microsoft but we are more likely to have eight out of twelve winners."

The group's tendency to bet on a person rather than a company and to choose to invest to see what happens is most difficult for Andrew Sachs, who, as the fund manager, would like to make money. Sachs, who screens the deals, sees 200 business plans a month. He says he won't have this job forever because the members like to have new deal-makers every few years. Members often "sponsor" presenters, a practice that tends to give the company an edge. But sponsorship does not convey a guarantee, and sometimes members are annoyed that their protégés are turned down. And the first person to speak up as a deal is being discussed has a lot of sway.

Members of the group acknowledge, proudly, that they're a tough audience. "Everyone has already had dinner, these young people come in, and we torture them," admits John Sidgmore. "Their whole life is up or down in ten minutes."

Short, curly-haired, intellectual David Holtzman, for years the top technologist at Internet domain name registrar Network Solutions, which assigns the *.com, .net,* and other Web addresses, stands giddily nervous in front of the group. AOL's Steve Case is there, so is Nasdaq executive Al Berkeley, and John Sidgmore of WorldCom. Holtzman already has funding for his new company, Opion, which measures buzz—of a movie, a stock, a person—on the Internet, but he wants a nod from these guys because of who they are and what they represent. He sweats through a presentation at the restaurant 1789 in Georgetown because he considers it a rite of passage to be approved by the club.

Pitching to the Capital Investors is like being in a Roman amphitheater, says Holtzman. "They're eating, drinking, then it's thumbs-up or thumbs-down. It's the lions and the Christians."

And Holtzman is one they liked—he got money.

"It gives you in one fell swoop more names to throw around than any individual investment," says John Burton. Still, after many of the companies threw around some names more than others—putting out press releases saying Steve Case and Marc Andreessen were their new investors when neither of them had even been at the meeting when the decision was made—the group created a rule that a portfolio company had to list each and every member of the Capital Investors if it listed one.

Every time Susan DeFife sees that royal blue suit in her closet—the one she wore in 1998 to present her company WomenCONNECT.com to the Capital Investors—she remembers that evening and then looks for something else to wear. It's funny, she hardly ever remembers what she wore at an event, but that particular outfit is so strongly linked to that dinner that she hasn't been able to put it on since.

It was a horrible, gut-wrenching experience asking the Capital Investors for money that night at the Ritz-Carlton in Tysons Corner. She remembers walking in and immediately losing her focus as she tried to calculate in her head the combined net worth in the room. As she began pitching her idea for a Web site that would create a community for working women, they were eating dessert and most were looking down at a copy of her business plan, presumably reading it for the first time. "I wanted to shake them and say, 'Are you listening or am I here for your amusement?'" says DeFife.

She considered the presentation a test: "How will she react if we hit her hard?" The group didn't invest.

Horrible, but also enlightening. The members were harsh but they brought up things she hadn't thought of. And while it seemed like a disaster at first, the meeting eventually became quite fruitful. One of the members, John Burton, was already an investor. Mark Warner invested after her presentation. Alan Spoon invited her over to *The Washington Post* to talk about her business, and Mario Morino introduced her to just about everyone in Washington she should know.

Burton says the group's decision not to invest in Women-CONNECT, which has since gone out of business, was one of its more rational ones. "Everybody loved Susan, but we'd seen the effort it takes to bring traffic to an affinity site," he says. DeFife made it a personal mission to prove him wrong. "The guy beat me to hell and back before I got his money," she says.

DeFife says the men won't call it this, but that in times of economic turmoil, Capital Investors has became a kind of support group. She understands that role of leaning on one another much better than their purpose of early stage investors. "I'm puzzled by what they've invested in," she says. "There doesn't seem to be a pattern or logic." She says the deflated portfolio is certainly "ego-bruising" to the group, much more painful than the small amounts of money they've lost.

DeFife herself belongs to RPW, also known as Rich Powerful Women, an all-female group of top Washington business people started by software executive Kathy Clark. At least three in the group, including DeFife, saw their companies crumble in the late 1990s. While RPW doesn't make angel investments, DeFife says it is similar to Capital Investors in many other ways. "Those are the people we all fall back on," says DeFife. "You learn real fast who will be there when you hit rock bottom."

CHAPTER THREE

MORTON'S, TYSONS CORNER, VIRGINIA

December 2000

As the group gathers in the dark wood-paneled room at Morton's, it's clear many members are distracted by falling stock prices. For the first time, it seems strange, almost indulgent, that they are here tonight at this steak house to help other companies. Some of their own businesses need saving, or selling. The negotiations are exhausting. They are tired, weary, depleted.

Fernandez talks solemnly about news that day that one of his arch-rivals has made enormous layoffs. His industry is being battered and it would soon be his turn to send out a flurry of pink slips. Funny how quickly a much-lamented workforce shortage had morphed into a workforce glut.

Mandl has his own problems. His president, Kirby "Buddy" Pickle, has just quit Teligent. The company's stock price has been decimated and Wall Street analysts are questioning its future. "Buddy wanted to be the CEO and I'm the CEO," says Mandl. He has a lot at stake: Mandl was considered to be the next in line for the top job at AT&T when he shocked the telecom industry by joining the little-known start-up.

"The marketplace will reflect the performance," Mandl says stoically. "The newer companies will suffer even more." The members settle in at two circular tables with fuchsia orchids in the center. Each ring begins its own quiet conversation, focusing on the decimation of the market and other people's fortunes.

Seeing one another for the first time since the presidential election was finally concluded, some disagree on the process. "It's like looking at art," says Fernandez. "I see one thing, you see another."

Wine is poured and the first course, little dishes of lump crabmeat, is served as Jonathan Silver introduces SwapDrive, a company that creates software that acts like a virtual file cabinet.

Everyone seems a bit surprised that the company is being ushered in so soon, before they'd had a chance to relax.

The SwapDrive presenter is low-key and talks in a conversational style. Nasdaq vice chairman Al Berkeley, WorldCom vice chairman John Sidgmore, and venture capitalist Art Marks all quiz him on the company.

"What do storage networks *do*?" asks Saylor tersely. He's not particularly impressed with the answer and continues, "They must do more than that," as he dips his crabmeat into a dish of tartar sauce.

"Would you characterize yourself as a *reseller*?" Saylor asks.

The presenter looks at him blankly. "Do you sell this stuff yourself?" asks Sidgmore in a gentler voice.

Warner is cutting bread for the table, spearing each piece with a fork and offering it to the guys.

Berkeley and Sidgmore start a private banter.

Another SwapDrive presenter starts to explain what *http* and *ftp* stand for. The members look amused.

All of a sudden the questions heat up. National Geographic's John Fahey, Proxicom founder Raul Fernandez, and Mandl jump in.

Everyone is talking at once.

"How much does it cost to buy ten gigabytes compared to one terabyte?" asks Saylor.

Time for the SwapDrive guys to leave.

Fahey leans in to Warner and asks, "Do you understand this? What's a gigabyte?" Warner laughs. Fahey, one of the few in the group without a technology background, often seems lost when the talk turns technical. Fahey generally pokes fun at himself in these instances.

"People will meet at shared storage," says Berkeley. "It's the vaporization of core infrastructure," he declares.

"I have trouble seeing the scale," says Greenfield.

"It's hard for me to see how they're going to break even," says Sidgmore.

"I don't see how they'll sell this inside a company," adds Saylor.

Saylor launches into a blitz so full of tech jargon phrases like *full duplex cad swap* that he is starting to sound like he's talking in another language, his words blurring. He does not pause for several minutes, his pace not allowing any interruptions.

And that's it, they all seem to have decided against SwapDrive.

"All right, Andrew, bring in the next," orders Warner.

Russ Ramsey introduces Amir Hudda, a serial entrepreneur in that this company, Emtera, is his second start-up. His first, Entevo, was sold to Bindview Corp. for $125 million at the beginning of 2000.

"Quite a few of you know me from my Entevo days," says Hudda, who is wearing a turtleneck and blazer. His first company's investors included venture funds affiliated with Marks and Ramsey.

Berkeley takes off his tie, folds it carefully, puts it in his suit pocket, and settles in for the speech.

Hudda's colleague explains how the technology allows a consumer to read product reviews on a wireless phone while simultaneously checking out the product at a store.

"Who do you sell to? The retail store or the portal?" asks software inventor Bill Gorog.

Dinner, a choice of filet mignon, salmon, or lamb chops, is served and a waitress walks around with a silver caddie full of sour cream, bacon bits, and butter for baked potatoes.

Everyone starts asking questions again, all at once.

"So who's going to pay for it?" asks Fernandez.

"Wouldn't it be easier if I gave BlackBerrys to my clerks?" says Saylor.

"Do you know about these robots in Richmond at Wal-Mart?" asks Berkeley. Saylor looks amused. "Danger, danger, Will Robinson," he says.

"This is the same conversation people had five years ago about kiosks," sniffs Greenfield, invoking the once-popular but now-dead idea that Internet "kiosks" should be installed in public places like malls and post offices so people could constantly check their email while on the move.

Warner's patience has clearly waned. He's ready to get to the point.

"How many people have you got? How much money have you raised? What are you looking for?" he fires off in staccato.

"No revenue yet?" asks Saylor.

And it's over. They all clap.

"We're like the Supreme Court," says Fahey.

"This is my area of expertise," announces Saylor. "Best Buy is my customer."

"And only yours," retorts Ramsey.

"I haven't seen this work. These guys don't know what they don't know," says Saylor.

"There is no way a billion-dollar retailer is going to spend a million on this model," agrees Fernandez. "Retailing for the next twelve months is not going anywhere."

They perk up slightly when a waiter brings in a special bottle of wine and begins showing it around. But it turns out the bottle was meant for someone else, and the waiter scurries away.

The Capital Investors are grouchy and annoyed. There is a third company scheduled to present, but the group has clearly lost its ability to concentrate or care.

"I pity the next company," says Warner.

"I pity the next victim," corrects Berkeley.

Mandl leaves to go to a Teligent dinner, living the life of a high-powered CEO who double-books all three meals of the day. No wonder so many need personal trainers. Saylor also gets up to go, leaving his fork standing straight up in his baked potato. Fahey quietly slips out.

In a brief discussion about the struggling Internet service provider PSINet, Sidgmore says he tried to buy the company several times, but PSINet founder Bill Schrader would never let him. It would be a bargain now, if such a deal could be approved by the government and shareholders.

Silver introduces Core Communications, which his venture firm has already backed with $2.9 million. McDonnell has $500,000 of his own cash in the deal, too. The presenter, CEO David Giannini, a tax lawyer, is slick and salesman-like. The team also includes a former chief technology officer and vice president of finance at Transaction Network Services with investment help from Melton.

"What kind of margin do you get?" asks Marks. "What's the first sales cycle like?"

"Make it local, make it real for us here," suggests Fernandez. Marks is writing on a napkin.

"If you sold everyone on your target rate, how much would your revenue be?" asks Sidgmore.

Warner has started handing out his new business cards to Walker, Fernandez, and Morino, who are all looking at the little pieces of paper.

The logo of Warner's investment fund, Columbia Capital, is on the top. But the front of the business card also includes a full-color cartoon of Warner drawn as a superhero. This version of Warner sports a half-smile and a wink and is forcefully connecting two Internet access lines, muscles bulging and tie flying up in the air. It's called an "EGO" card, which officially stands for "Everyone's Got One," designed by a graphics team in Richmond. Flip over the card and you'll find Warner's superhero name, ".gov," and his vital statistics and details about which evils he fights against. (".gov represses a fear of low bandwidth and ivory towers.") His height is listed as "towering" and his origin as "the 'new' old dominion." Not surprisingly, strength and stamina charts show him to be at "5," the top level.

Warner looks up long enough to ask, "How much are you looking for?"

Silver jumps in, saying the round has actually already been raised, but his venture firm Core Capital would back off a chunk if the group was interested.

Everyone claps and Sachs leads them away.

"I like this company. I like the guy, too," says Sidgmore.

Warner is bored. It's been an evening heavy with presentations and light on general banter among the group. "Let's talk about more important things," he says.

"I've got questions about the long-term market," says Marks.

Still, a Sidgmore nod carries weight and no one seems in the mood for a long discussion.

"You feel like the CEO knows what he's doing," agrees Greenfield.

Silver tries to talk up the first company, saying the presenter didn't do a great job of explaining what SwapDrive does. Silver's venture capital firm has invested in this company, too, and Capital Investor John Burton is about to join SwapDrive's board of directors, but the decision is already made.

Everyone is eating strawberries and cake.

Warner is ready to get the decisions over with. "Up on number three? Done. Contestant number two? Thumbs-down. Contestant number one? Thumbs-down."

"Any fun plans for the holidays?" Warner continues. Marks is going to New York to see four Broadway shows, Greenfield and Ramsey are both traveling to Aspen.

"You'll be out begging again," Sidgmore says to Warner.

Berkeley talks about a Civil War reenactment coming up he'd like the group to watch.

Several members start talking about how every day it seems Warner is having a fund-raiser, every minute he's thinking about building that campaign war chest.

Warner says, "Andrew, why don't you give us some end of the year cheer?"

"What are *you* going to do next?" asks Marks, before Sachs can reply.

"I'm waiting for offers," responds Sachs.

Sidgmore mentions that all three presenters are waiting at the bar to hear their verdicts, maybe they should move along. But now Warner wants a portfolio update.

"Generally speaking, we're doing okay, no pigs in the poke, right?" asks Warner.

"We'll have some problems," admits Sachs. "We should brace. There will be some that will run out of money."

Sachs explains that Cyveillance and EqualFooting have made layoffs. Another investee company, KnowledgeMax, is out looking for money again. The group needs to decide whether it will re-invest in any of the companies in its portfolio, something it so far has not done. Warner asks Sachs to send an email to the members about that possibility, then checks himself.

"The read-rate on email in this group is low," Warner says. The question still hangs in the air as the members leave the private room.

Two of the presenting groups are having their own dinner out in the main dining room of the steak house, a third is in the bar. Fernandez and Morino, who is on the board of Proxicom, take their own spot at the bar to catch up.

Sachs visits each of the teams and gives them the news. No. No. Yes. Sachs says if he's learned anything running this fund, it's that he can never predict what the group is going to decide on something. And it's certainly not easy explaining a no, or even a yes, sometimes, to the eager start-up executives waiting.

CHAPTER FOUR

THE HEYDAY

ROUND SEVEN O'CLOCK one morning in 1997, Mario Morino stood before 100 would-be entrepreneurs and told them if they were serious about starting a company, they should all tape two words to their bathroom mirrors and look at them every day: Ego and Greed.

Morino explained that when he worried about getting his institute off the ground, an adviser told him, "If we fail we have no problem. If we succeed we have two problems—ego and greed. These are the only two things that will ever hold us back." It became known as the "ego and greed speech," and as the small technology community grew, it was repeated and changed and listened to like a parable. But it was guidance that was so common sense, and in euphoric boom times it eventually became white noise. The advice whirred in the background, but few were listening.

Instead, they were much too busy trying to figure out how to get into this Internet thing. There was a scent of money in the air and a palpable feeling that things were about to change. Instead of having a screenplay or the great American novel in their back pocket, it seemed everyone had an Internet company idea written on a paper napkin. And they were waiting to be discovered by a venture capitalist. The investors offered millions for vague ideas and threw money at numerous concepts, hoping something would stick. And much of it did. The mantra was "Get big fast or go home." The holy grail was a "disruptive" technology, one that would change the way we live and work. Like the Web, like email, and not, it turns out, like online dry-cleaning or selling pet food on the Internet. But it would take some time to learn such things.

Just several years before, those who talked about computers and communications networks as technologies that would alter our lives were laughed at, or at least thought to be incredible bores.

Now, they were becoming high-drama.

"They come to our market and plan out their victories and their tragedies," says Nasdaq vice chairman and Capital Investor Al Berkeley. "It's a stage."

Back in the quieter times, in the spring of 1995 at a meeting of business leaders, Morino told the group about his idea to create the Potomac KnowledgeWay Project, a think tank to help Washington grow as a technology center. And Steve Case spoke about the future of his company, America Online, then just one of the three largest online service providers, continually battling with Prodigy and CompuServe for customers. Morino and Case were, even then, on the fringes of Washington's business community.

Morino, called the "godfather" by Washington entrepreneurs, built that think tank, although he ran into trouble raising money for it over the years. He also created a building where high-tech tenants would work under the same roof and where he would hold events to introduce the right people to one another. At the same time, Case built AOL. For Washington start-up entrepreneurs, the community-minded Morino and company-focused Case became role models. And through most of AOL's history, it was an insular company. Its leaders focused on themselves rather than on the geography around them. For years, they were criticized for ignoring their hometown, but were forgiven for their ultimate success. While the Internet was supposed to make physical location irrelevant, it turned out that like car dealers that cluster on a city block, a critical mass of technology businesses can bring new life and economic prosperity to an area.

As regions across the country sprouted technology communities—Boston, New York, North Carolina—each had a person or a group of people who acted as the connectors. Those people introduced those who should know one another, served as cheerleaders and sometime critics, and became their town centers personified.

In Washington, Morino is that glue. Morino does favors for many of the hordes of people who come to him for help finding a job, a donation, an introduction.

"Where he goes, he creates in human terms what computers do," says Liz Wainger, a former employee of Morino's.

One day he said he planned to "pulse out" to the community that a certain person had lost their job and wanted the right new position, not just any job. Like Marlon Brando and then Al Pacino in the movie, people line up to ask for Morino's help. The difference is that the line is in his email box. People are also afraid to cross this man with the puppy-dog eyes and receding hairline. Several employees at his nonprofit Morino Institute who wanted to find a new job found they had to openly put themselves on the market with Morino's blessing. Otherwise, no company would have chanced to steal one of Mario's people. And though his other nickname is "Saint Mario," he can hold a grudge.

"Certain people are using you, so you use them in return and you never let them forget it," he says.

Morino is insulted when it is suggested that he has arrived where he has because of money. When The Brookings Institution asked him to join their board in 2001, he asked why. If Brookings just wanted money, he didn't want its leaders to pretend to listen to his ideas. If the institution wanted his name to put on promotional material to attract other techies, the same thing applied. But Brookings insisted they wanted his brain, not his cash or connections, so Morino joined.

Thirsty for advice, new entrepreneurs flocked to Morino's speeches, but at first, they couldn't understand a word he said. His thoughts moved faster than his mouth could accommodate. He learned to speak slower after an aide started taping a sign that said *Slow down, Mario,* to the podium. (Marc Andreessen, who had a similar problem, hired a speech coach to keep him from disappointing the crowds that expected to hear clear words of wisdom.)

How Morino came to this role is the subject of *The Journey* a memoir posted on the Netpreneur Web site. Few of his fans have read it. As telling as the story is, it's convoluted enough that a public relations person purposely made it difficult to find on the site.

Growing up in a poor section of Cleveland where he learned what he calls a "streetfighter" mentality, Morino thought he'd be a math teacher and baseball coach. Instead, he co-founded a software firm called Morino Associates that, through a series of acquisitions, became Legent Corp. Morino retired in 1992, but was still a large stockholder and board member when Legent was sold to Computer Associates in 1995. He made about $100 million from the sale.

In 1993, Morino began what he calls the "discovery process." He and a friend, Patrick Arnone, spent that year and part of the next on a road trip, traversing the country to talk with congressmen, educators, religious leaders, business people, and others. Topics of conversation were computer networks, community, and whatever else came up. More pilgrims than prophets, they had no agenda, no goal, and no plan. By the end of the year-and-a-half sojourn, they had met with 700 people.

Some days meetings would be enlightening, other days they would encounter people suspicious of what Morino and Arnone were doing. Just what exactly was it they were selling?

While Morino was gone, meanwhile, those back at the Institute were not only wondering what he was doing, but what they were supposed to be working on themselves. Morino had put the group on hold while he thought things through. His thoroughness has frustrated colleagues who are used to having a specific assignment that doesn't get analyzed for years before it's begun. Morino has a tendency to study things to death, to overanalyze. "Anything that appears to be a whim is not a whim," says Morino.

When he returned from the discovery phase, Morino launched the Potomac KnowledgeWay Project, so-named for the "knowledge" economy base in Washington. That group created the Netpreneur Program and became a local clearinghouse for people trying to understand the information age. Morino poured his own money into this project—$1 million to start and then about $1.5 million annually in the four years since the launch—and enlisted friends such as Russ Ramsey and Mark Warner to serve on the board.

Morino's protégés, the netpreneurs, were direct descendants of Washington's first wave of Internet and telecom success, America Online, UUNet, MCI WorldCom, and Network Solutions. Some had worked at these companies; others were inspired by them.

The KnowledgeWay's most successful branch, the Netpreneur Program, held regular "Coffee and DoughNets" sessions in the mornings and evening events with themes and popular speakers. It brought like-minded people together the way Capital Investors did. But unlike Capital Investors, no one was shut out. It fostered inclusion—events were free and open to anyone up to the legal limit of the venue for attendance, which was often reached. Food and drink were free, too, at most of the events, an easy enticement for hungry techies.

While early meetings might have attracted 100 people, the gatherings began to draw more than 1,000 when there was an especially interesting speaker. It was at Netpreneur where Washington technologists came out of the woodwork.

At the end of the evening, after the presentations were over and the lights were dimmed, the entrepreneurs would keep talking to one another. They were forced into the hallway by the cleanup crew, then moved over to the bar, and often out into the street where they would share venture capital search stories and compare technologies until somebody's spouse interrupted with a cell phone call.

Along the way, Morino's beliefs and suggestions became part of the mythology of the region. Besides the "ego and greed" speech, there was the idea of finding the right mentor, then becoming a mentor. And, increasingly, there was Morino's view on philanthropy, which, like many of the high-tech class, he calls "giving back."

Perhaps especially in Washington, a focus on something creative, anything other than dreary politics, seemed incredibly refreshing. People like punk rocker David Levine and former

CIA agent Greg Keough were more passionate about their start-ups than anything else they'd ever done. Those who were disillusioned with the government, who had always felt like outsiders in a one-tune town, found in technology something they could finally get excited about. And maybe they'd make some money along the way. Business people even came to Washington to start companies, not just to lobby for political favors. It wasn't just all Internet; biotech, fiber optics, and telecom firms sprouted up.

"I have to schedule breakfasts and lunches so I eat," said an energized and frenetically busy Elliott Frutkin, the twenty-something CEO of Web design firm Doceus, Inc. Looking back, of course, it's clear many of these pioneers saw their future through rose-colored glasses. But at the time everyone was having too much fun and working way too hard to notice.

There was an unofficial blueprint for how to build a technology capital that was passed around the country. First, they would need a blockbuster company, preferably a household name, that would make employees rich and inspired enough to start other companies and encourage entrepreneurship just by being successful. That, of course, was America Online. Then there should be a group to help build the community—the Netpreneur Program. There should also be access to all stages of venture capital, from the maxed-out credit stage to just before going public. Funds for the different life cycles of a company were created in Washington and branches of firms from around the country moved to the region, in search of good deals. The mix would have empathetic "service providers," those lawyers, accountants, and real estate brokers who would understand why a start-up needs a flexible, short-term lease and who might take equity in place of cash in payment for their services. Those, too, grew up in Washington, with Silicon Valley banks and law firms opening offices in the region. With these attributes, says venture capitalist and Capital Investor Art Marks, you have the "engine that hums." In the early days, the two biggest problems facing technologists were not enough venture capital money to fund new companies and not enough workers to make them run.

But abruptly, a few good public offerings and a wildly increasing interest of the average person in technology and the stock market forced change. Everyone wanted to be cutting-edge and everyone wanted to be rich.

Fear of missing out forced the ecosystem to broaden. The rest of Washington wanted to cash in on the new rich and get to know them better. Charities cultivated them, real estate agents courted them, and—much to their surprise—technologists became the most sought after people at social events and bene-fits. They had lots of money, they were young, and many were fun, although it was clear quite a few had ignored Morino's ego-and-greed advice. The Phillips Collection, an art museum, held fund-raising events for the tech elite, inviting many of the Cap-ital Investors. After cocktails in one gallery and before the museum tour began, a Phillips representative said the techies should have much in common with the Phillips—they were not of government Washington or Smithsonian Washington, but of independent Washington. The venture capitalists, too, became like town celebrities, and because the top ones saw all the deals in town, they knew all the best gossip.

Steve Zarpas, who grew up in Virginia thinking the stretch of land from Washington to Dulles was just a sleepy green pasture, watched the region bloom. He'd recently shut down the Crow Bar downtown and was casting about for the next thing. He saw the techies as a great unmet challenge. Zarpas and Ed Andrews opened the Revolution Coffee Lounge in Herndon in 1999 to cater to the techies. They had T1 lines next to bar stools and held "Tech Thursday" events.

Investing clubs and other technology networking groups served as social interaction during the rise. People heard about the Capital Investors, and they began forming other dinner clubs around the city. Technology salons—some were investing clubs and others were social circles—proliferated. One was called the "Brat Pack," a group of under-thirty technology leaders who gathered for beer and sympathy. Most of the members were early, early stage—meaning no profits, few customers, and sometimes no product. They asked one another basic questions that only new CEOs would have, like "How much do we pay ourselves?" They talked about girlfriends (they were mostly male and single) and raising venture capital. At one meeting, Elie Ashery, co-founder of Newsletters.com (which later struggled and was sold), stood up at the Third Edition bar in George-town and declared that the group should start "giving back." He suggested the members donate stock to charity and coach high school students in how to start a business. The members nod-ded. This was, after all, the mantra they heard from Morino. Never mind that most of them didn't have fully formed compa-nies yet. Ashery said later that he brought up the subject because he was influenced by Morino, whom he has only briefly met. "I feel like the community has really given me a lot," he says. "And Mario is the reason."

Morino is pleased to hear this story, but it doesn't surprise him. The goal all along was to bring the community full circle, so the companies he helped would help someone else. Morino himself would never have been that twenty-something looking to give back, though. He was too busy building his company then. Some of the businesses that benefited most from Netpre-neur, like Ashery's company and WomenCONNECT.com, run by Susan DeFife, faded away. It remains to be seen if Morino's influence will carry through to their next endeavors.

Still, Morino's presence in the technology community of Washington is so forceful that a kind of meltdown happens every August when he, his wife, and children go to Bethany Beach for two or three weeks. It's known as Morino's "under-ground" time. He does not answer calls, emails, faxes, pages, or any non-emergency communication whatsoever. It's family time and if you want to reach him, you can't do it then.

Morino has had detached summer vacations annually since 1993 and considers them essential to those like him who are always "on." However, he admits: "When I disconnect, I don't want to come back."

After networking events, Morino is swarmed by young entrepreneurs. Unlike some speakers who seem only to give advice, he also asks questions and files things away in his own thoughts. "Mario is a sponge, but a selective sponge," says Mary McPherson, who runs the Netpreneur Program and often ushers Morino through the crowds at these events.

Without Morino, a tech-oriented community would have emerged in Washington on its own in some way, but his influence and investment shaped it in a certain form and created it much faster. Still, there was no community center, a focal point of the sort people are drawn to in great cities.

So the next grand plan was to design a building, loosely based on 55 Broad Street in New York, that would become a high-tech nexus. It would house companies and their funders and foster an entrepreneurial spirit in the hallways and cafeteria. Morino didn't know exactly what would happen in these common spaces, and that was fine.

It was called "11600 Sunrise" because of its location on Sunrise Valley Drive in Reston. It sounded like a name for a television soap opera, and indeed, young beautiful people played pool in the chill-out room and chased dot-com dreams. Of course, no one called it 11600 Sunrise. It was the

"Morino Building" or "Planet Mario," or to many, simply "The Building."

The idea to create a high-tech hothouse stemmed in part from Morino's frustration with the conservative ways of technology companies in Washington. The Washington-centric businesses of law, public policy, and government contracting didn't exactly encourage a creative atmosphere for techies. "The Washington region's been buttoned down," Morino said. "To get people really working hard, you've got to have fun. They're going to be there all night . . ."

The idea was pushed along by Morino's conversations with his friend Raul Fernandez, one of the youngest members of the Capital Investors. For years, the two had talked about moving their companies into the same space to see what they would learn from each other.

David Holtzman, former top technologist at Network Solutions and founder of start-up Opion, says what Morino has done for the community is to create an environment where things are possible.

Morino put $20 million of his own money into the renovations—$5 million up front and $15 million from a bank loan. No lawyers, accountants, or other "service providers" were allowed space, although there are four times as many parking spaces as tenants to encourage outsiders to visit.

The problem with the house that Mario built is that it takes its creator a half hour to go on a bagel run to the cafeteria. It takes him so long to get his breakfast because he gets swamped by people who want to talk to him.

The building became a must-see stop on a tour of high-tech Washington. Other spots included the Dulles headquarters of AOL and Network Solutions in Reston, where most domain names are registered. But a foreign delegation, or congressman, or out-of-town techie like Jim Barksdale or Esther Dyson, looking to "see" technology in Washington, would often just spend a day at 11600 Sunrise.

It is a central point, too, for the Capital Investors. Fernandez's company offices are in the building. Bill Gorog's InteliData is, too, as well as the venture capital arm for Friedman, Billings, Ramsey Group (FBR).

When Mark Warner was looking for the perfect place for an initial extravaganza fund-raiser to hit up techies for campaign contributions, 11600 Sunrise was the obvious choice. Supporters needed merely to walk from their offices or make a quick jaunt from Tysons Corner.

The network effect of the building comes not from planned events but from the organic way people do business in the hallways, overhear tech gossip in the chill-out room, or swap insights on the treadmills.

"It's like an old neighborhood," says Morino. "When I see someone connecting I get excited." It's what the inhabitants call "Living the Building."

Those who didn't have a particular reason to come to

11600 Sunrise would just drop by, hoping to run into venture capitalists. John Backus, managing director of venture capital fund Draper Atlantic at 11600 Sunrise, walked out of the men's room one day to find someone waiting with a business plan for him. Backus trained his assistants to keep out the droppers-by. They can deliver their plans, but shouldn't expect an instant meeting.

A visiting North Carolina company also saw the bathroom as a high-profile spot. Its marketers plastered business cards on the walls inside all the bathrooms in the building. It was hard to forget their name, building occupants agreed.

"I don't have to go meet anyone anymore," says Fran Witzel of the Netpreneur Program. "Everyone wants to come to the building."

The building is quiet in early morning when the mist has barely cleared from the lot of luxury cars with their Virginia vanity license plates. This is workout time for the techie population. Televisions in front of each of thirteen stairmasters and treadmills are dutifully tuned to CNBC. In the building's restaurant, Via Cucina, people are ordering coffee. Some tenants have a deal with the café that lets all their employees eat for free. Others are on their own.

The techies bring their coffee to their office or sit at one of the tiny red tables, staring at the colorful mural that was created by the tenants at the building's opening party. There are spray-painted names and logos and slogans like *Don't take a job, make a job,* and *Love what you do.* A picture of an island declares *Entrepreneur Oasis.*

Well, it was for a brief shining moment. As the market fell apart, so did some of the tenant companies. FBR's two top venture capitalists walked out unexpectedly one day after disagreements with the parent company. Others had better luck. CyberMark was sold; Updata Capital (run by Capital Investor John Burton) got too big for its space and moved out to larger offices.

In the middle of the day, the chill-out room is used as the "closing room." People hiring, doing deals, or wooing someone take their prospects there to sit under the neon *Rock the House* sign next to the bar and game tables. One of Proxicom's employees is there in the middle of the day, playing pool. He says he comes up at least twice a day to "clear his mind."

It's party time one evening in the chill-out room, which has a beer tap (this night's vintage is Vistranet Lager, named after one of the tenants), jukebox, gigantic television screen, and pre-requisite foosball table. "Have a seat on the Caddy and grab a beer, this is my office," says Christie Hart, marketing manager for venture capital firm Draper Atlantic, pointing at a seat that's shaped like a Cadillac. The room quickly becomes crowded with young men and women holding plastic beer cups and playing air hockey under the neon signs; they seem more like college students than technology workers. But there are clues. As they lean over for pool shots you can spot the cell phones, Black-Berrys, and pagers strapped to their belts like secret weapons.

"I totally covet this building," says Jamey Harvey, founder of iKimbo, between heated foosball games. He says he drops by every couple of days to eat lunch or hang out. Sometimes Harvey is visiting his bankers and venture capitalists who are in the building, but often he comes just to schmooze. As a guest, though, he's trying to figure out just what level of networking is okay. "I can't figure out if I can recruit people here," he says, looking around quizzically at the young workers.

On another afternoon, the chill-out room is home to the Washington version of *Who Wants to be a Millionaire?*, with a healthy dose of reality thrown in. While it seemed everyone was starting an Internet company, not everyone was hooked into the venture capital network, and financiers gave most attention to deals sent to them by personal recommendations. So Draper Atlantic and the Netpreneur Program began holding a fun monthly event called FastPitch that democratizes the process by letting just about anyone pitch an idea. On a particular day, eighteen executives have come to 11600 Sunrise to give one-minute presentations. Narrowed to nine, they compete again. The grand prize winner gets an hour of advice from Fran Witzel, vice president of the Netpreneur Program, plus a meeting with Draper Atlantic. Actually, this game is more like "Sorry, You're Not Going to Be a Millionaire." Some are told bluntly not to quit their day jobs.

John Backus of Draper Atlantic tells pitchers: "If you're passionate about changing the world, you might make money. If you're passionate about making money, you won't."

It was a regular occurrence in the late 1990s for Backus to ask an entrepreneur what his dreams were and hear "to make $10 million." Or $20 million. For many, it was not a search for better technology but a search for cash. Still, people were making it, which encouraged the rest. Secretaries and workers at all levels of companies like WorldCom and AOL became paper millionaires. AOL began holding seminars in financial planning for the newly rich employees, and fresh tract mansions filled the Washington suburbs.

The laminated bar counter in the chill-out room serves as a reminder of changing times. On opening night, guests wrote sayings, drew pictures, and predicted the future with blue, red, green, and pink markers. There are names of companies no longer alive. And . . .

Go Mario!

What a sandbox

Can I work here?

Show me the money

To the Godfather

It all starts here

Mario—You da man

You can sleep when you die.

And in small black letters at the bottom of one counter panel, almost like a whisper:

I hope this works.

But Morino wasn't the only one working on the next generation. As they became multimillionaires, and some billionaires, in the late 1990s, the Capital Investors began to encourage a new wave of Internet entrepreneurs through cash infusions and advice. And they began to anoint their favorites, extending their help and sometimes an invitation to join the club.

Paula Jagemann made her millions as John Sidgmore's secretary at UUNet. Jagemann put herself through college, did her final paper on UUNet's initial public offering, and started her own Internet venture, selling office supplies online. Sidgmore signed on as chairman of that company and her top investor and adviser.

As things were heating up, the Capital Investors chose Fernandez and Michael Saylor, CEO of MicroStrategy, both in their early thirties, to join their circle. While many of the older Capital Investors had stepped back a bit in their careers, they wanted to advise and learn from the newer guard. MicroStrategy had gone public in 1998, Proxicom in 1999. Both men were single until Fernandez married in June of 2000, and they were often compared to each other, and sometimes confused with each other.

Fernandez has an uncanny ability to meet experienced advisers, impress them with his respectful attitude and energetic curiosity, and make them his lifelong supporters. Fernandez built his board that way, adding former boss Jack Kemp, Morino, and AOL executive Ted Leonsis as directors. Proxicom attracted huge clients like General Motors and, of course, AOL. It opened offices around the world and made a lot of people wealthy, especially Fernandez. Many of the BMWs and Mercedes in the Morino building parking lot were owned by Proxicom's new rich. Vanity license plates, like "STOKOPT" and the company's ticker, "PXCM", abounded.

Fernandez, along with Leonsis, Mathias, and Ramsey, joined an investor group of sixty-some politicians, technologists, and financiers to open a restaurant called The Caucus Room, a clubby steakhouse-type place that would be a downtown meeting place for players of each world.

But it was a deal brokered by Leonsis with Michael Jordan that really made the rest of Washington notice that technology—and high-tech wealth—was changing the region's economy and culture.

In 1999, Leonsis and several other partners created Lincoln Holdings, a sports ownership group that owns the NHL's Washington Capitals and stakes in the NBA's Washington Wizards, the WBNA's Washington Mystics, the MCI Center and US Airways Arena, and Ticketmaster/Citysearch. Part of that deal with sports impresario Abe Pollin gives Leonsis the right to buy the remaining shares of the franchises and stadiums whenever Pollin is ready to sell, or when Pollin dies.

A few months after the deal, Leonsis was looking for a way to create big buzz for the teams. He was frustrated that Washington wasn't considered much of a sports town, and he was accustomed to the high-profile success of AOL. There was no way he would stand to be a behind-the-scenes third-rate sports owner. Leonsis wanted championships, celebrations, and huge stars.

Over lunch at the Capital Grille in September of 1999, Leonsis told his partners he was going after Michael Jordan. They laughed. But a few weeks later, after a flurry of talks with Jordan's agent, David Falk, Leonsis would be flying his private jet to lunch with Jordan at the basketball star's restaurant, one sixtyblue. It turned out that Jordan wanted to run operations of a franchise and that he was fascinated with the Internet and what technology could do for business. He was taking Leonsis quite seriously.

For the next couple of months, negotiations ensued. Leonsis, Jordan, George Stamas, and Jordan's two agents met again in November at the St. Regis Hotel in midtown Manhattan. At one point Jordan ordered a bottle of 1961 Chateaux Latour, a Bordeaux that costs about $3,000. The basic understanding was that Jordan's investment in Lincoln Holdings would reach 20 percent of the company. But Jordan could only run basketball operations when Pollin retired. That wasn't what Jordan wanted. So after that meeting disbanded, Leonsis set about to get Pollin to sign on to the deal. In December, Pollin and Jordan met at Pollin's Bethesda home. Pollin wanted Wes Unseld, the head of basketball operations for the Wizards, to be treated well and to keep an important role.

At the same time, Leonsis was arranging to buy out one of Pollin's minority partners to increase Lincoln Holdings' stake of Pollin's company, known as Washington Sports, to 44 percent. Leonsis, building his own team, would then bring in his friend Raul Fernandez.

In mid-January of 2000, early in the morning, Jordan phoned Leonsis at his Great Falls home. Yes, he was coming to Washington.

The owner's box of the Washington Capitals immediately became a power center of the city, one of the first places where politicians, sports stars, and technology executives mixed as equals.

Leonsis says they'll use everything they know as high-tech executives to develop a successful sports franchise. "I view these assets as being brands and media properties," says Leonsis.

General Alexander Haig, former secretary of state and a longtime AOL board member, dropped by the box one night; Chelsea Clinton another. Stamas, an investment banker who also became a Lincoln Holdings partner, is usually there, too, disappearing down the private elevator with someone or other to do a deal. On nights when Michael Jordan is in the box, the crowd is smaller, letting him have more breathing room.

As the technology community grew and Fernandez

emerged as a strong representative of his generation, Leonsis, Morino, and Kimsey took him under their wings. Those who benefited most from the Internet boom of the 1990s, like the thirty-five-year-old Fernandez, possessed an innate ability to find and make luck and to always show up at the right time and place. Fernandez didn't just have a good sense of timing, but an instinct to grab an opportunity at the right moment, like a terrier, and never let it go.

In 1988, a decade before the Internet boom, young congressional aide Raul Fernandez sat in a hotel room watching his boss, Jack Kemp, lose the Republican presidential primary, taking Fernandez's dreams of a State Department job down with him. Fernandez began thinking of leaving politics, maybe going into business. That day, Kemp asked the then twenty-two-year-old Fernandez to drive Henry Kissinger home from the Rayburn Office Building. In the elevator to the parking garage, the elder statesman counseled against abandoning politics. "Washington is a very lonely place when you don't have any power," he warned.

Fernandez now thinks that Kemp's loss is one of the luckiest moments of his life, and what Kissinger said to him is an odd prophecy. Who could know that the tech elite in Washington would eventually combine the old currency of power with that of cash?

"The world totally changed," says Fernandez. "Timing is everything." And somewhere along the way, a guy with a not particularly original idea—building Web sites for businesses—partnered with Michael Jordan, appeared on Fortune's forty richest under the age of forty list, and spoke during prime time at the Republican National Convention.

His first big break came on an airplane when he sat a row behind Ted Leonsis. Fernandez had no idea who Leonsis was, but overheard him saying that nobody really "got" the Web. "Maybe I could help," Fernandez said as he leaned over the airplane seat. Leonsis liked his chutzpah and signed on as Proxicom's first big client, hiring Fernandez to design an early version of the AOL.com site.

Fernandez is a born salesman—in high school he painted and installed new radios in used cars and sold them for a good profit—and networker, but is different from some technology executives because he honed his skills in the political world. It's a world where a group like Capital Investors makes even more sense, because friends and enemies like to keep each other close. Many of the members of Capital Investors, including Mario Morino, Jim Kimsey, and Russ Ramsey, have a personal "chief of staff" who acts as a point person for the boss. Ramsey's staffer holding that role, Phil Caplan, was previously staff secretary for President Bill Clinton.

At Proxicom, it sometimes feels as though the company is on a never-ending political campaign. Fernandez gives what he calls an annual "state of the union" address to his employees and holds quarterly "town halls" in each major office. At company headquarters in the Morino building, conference rooms are named "White House" and "Smithsonian."

"You've got to sell a vision, which is political," says Fernandez. "You've got to make sure that vision is current. Those are skills that guys who run our country have to have. A lot of it is transferable."

The work of a sports owner, too, is political. In the owner's box of the Capitals, Fernandez rarely sits down. He's making sure everyone has a drink, or the best view of the game, or has met someone he should get to know. "You've got to kiss babies and shake hands," Fernandez says of owning a team. "You have to master the art of talking, listening, and cheering."

As Fernandez was meeting AOL, so was the rest of the world.

On a summery day at America Online's first office in Vienna, Virginia, Steve Case brought back his arm slowly and threw with perfect aim and force to dunk William Razzouk, a man who was briefly in the No. 2 spot at AOL. It was family day at AOL, and employees were eating ice-cream cones and sauntering by the dunking machine set up to one side.

And again, over and over. Slam. Dunk. Slam. Dunk. Five or six times the flustered, pale Razzouk pulled himself out of the water and sat for more punishment as the entire AOL staff and their families pointed and laughed.

The message was clear: Steve Case was not going to let anyone mess up his plan. Razzouk was gone within weeks. "He was working the crowd," says Holidae Hayes, who remembers the moment well because it was a rare departure from Case's infamous steely composure. "He was not a blank tablet."

Razzouk was not fitting into the AOL hierarchy, and he had to go. But Case wasn't merely looking for a yes-man. Razzouk's replacement, Bob Pittman, helped fill in gaps caused by Case's inexperience. He was tolerated by Case because he made AOL stronger, and ultimately the two fashioned the company that was able to buy Time Warner just before the technology market fell apart.

Dunking Razzouk was also a physical manifestation of Case's relentless focus in creating AOL. The company made huge changes, going from an hourly billing structure to a monthly rate and trading its walled service for a gateway to the Internet. But Case's preachy message never changed, whether he was speaking to high school students, techies at an Internet World Convention, or theorists at an economic club dinner. Whenever he was in public, Case would give a version of the "building a medium we can be proud of" speech.

He called 2000 the "Internet Century" and young people in high school at that time the "Internet Generation." He was playing Internet philosopher way before most others. "You should take the lessons the Internet teaches and try to integrate them into whatever you do," he advised a graduating class.

Case's goal, his search, was never just to build the top Internet service provider in the world. More than anyone in the Capital Investors, his way of influencing social change is through his company. Through AOL, Case wants to dominate the way we communicate, live, work, and play.

AOL officially stated its plan to become the operating system for world communications when it launched its "AOL Anywhere" strategy.

The goal is to be in every home, car, purse, and back pocket, a mission that sounds insidious because AOL wants to be everywhere you are. Critics said it's creepy; AOL said it's convenient. What AOL did for Washington is to give it a blue-chip household name technology company to call its own. But AOL critics, including competitors like Earthlink and former volunteers on the site who feel slighted by the company, contend that AOL wants to be Big Brother. It has never pretended to be anything else.

"We just want to give people as many choices as possible in the hope that people more often than not pick one of our brands," says Case. "In a world of almost infinite choices, people will seek simplicity, integration, and convenience."

According to former AOL executives, one suggestion that never moved much beyond the memo stage was for AOL to buy the five major papers in the country: *The New York Times, The Washington Post, The Wall Street Journal, USA Today,* and the *Los Angeles Times,* thereby giving it control over newspaper readers nationwide. Pulling off that particular acquisition spree seems highly unlikely, but the fact that it was on paper at one time shows how the company works. In fact, at AOL there has been a constantly evolving "shopping list" circulated to the senior managers.

During the late 1990s, AOL seemed to do a deal a day, whether buying Netscape, CompuServe, MapQuest, or ICQ, or just forming a marketing agreement. Asked about the latest rumor, one exasperated executive finally said, "We are talking to everyone."

"It's like a geopolitical map of seventeenth-century Europe where all the daughters are being married off," says Kimsey about AOL's complicated and vast partnerships and planned takeovers.

AOL was attempting to show to its advertisers that it had captured the mass media audience. Actually, for AOL, there would be no point in selling if it were not to the masses, who would influence one another, pay reliable monthly fees, and also draw in the big bucks as advertising bait. In his speeches, Case became fond of listing his high-tech Ten Commandments, the first of which was, "The Mass Market Consumer Is Thy Master."

Every industry starts this way, explained Pittman, including the automobile industry. Then there's consolidation and only three or so survivors. "Before there was a mass market here, [Case] built this company as if the mass market was coming," said Pittman. "And for many years it looked like a dumb idea."

When asked in December of 1998 to name his single favorite moment of the year, Case pointed to the release of the movie *You've Got Mail*, a sweet, improbable tale of Internet love starring Meg Ryan and Tom Hanks. Not buying Netscape, not becoming the first Internet company to be listed in the S&P 500 stock index, but *You've Got Mail*. The movie was criticized as a new low in product placement, but Case was enormously proud. "It's a sign we're starting to have an impact on everyday life," he said.

The day the Starr Report was released, 800,000 people downloaded the report from AOL. When the former Princess Diana died, the system was overloaded. Somewhere along the line, people began to think of AOL as the Internet. And those same people began to hate it, too, because they depended on it. When AOL didn't have enough technical capacity to handle users, people who couldn't access their email were furious at the service.

Even though AOL was taunted by West Coast techies and others for being the Internet on training wheels, it legitimized Washington's claim to being a technology capital.

In early 1999, AOL formed a political action committee (PAC) for the region's tech industry. Called CapNet, it's a PAC that tries to influence legislative and regulatory decision making in favor of local companies. George Vradenburg took the lead for AOL on that project, saying the community needed a political voice. It was a calculated business move, not an act of charity.

"Long-term, we'll grow better, we'll be richer, if the ecosystem in which we live is better," says Vradenburg.

At about that time, Vradenburg said Washington technology was beginning to look a lot like his previous home, Hollywood, where actors, producers, and directors move from project to project with loyalty to the industry rather than to a job or company.

Washington was certainly attracting more stars, including Marc Andreessen, who became AOL's chief technology officer after his company, Netscape, was acquired by the Dulles giant. Andreessen bought a mansion in McLean, moved two of his three bulldogs there, joined the Capital Investors, and began to find restaurants he likes, such as Bertucci's on Leesburg Pike. But the bulldogs struggled through Washington summers and their owner never took to the AOL environment. Less than a year later, Andreessen announced he was leaving full-time work at AOL and moving back to California.

As AOL prospered, it seemed that at least half of Washington had an AOL employee, user of the service, or investor—or all three—under its roof. AOL's public relations team was notoriously closed-lipped about employee details. But executives allowed that AOL "paper" millionaires numbered in the thousands when the stock was high. At least a dozen of the company's top executives set up personal or family philanthropic foundations, a huge change from the pattern of retiring first, charity later.

Still, said Case, "Part of my job is to delegate paranoia and worry."

As Case grew his empire, the Capital Investors saw their goal of attracting outside money to Washington fulfilled.

In 1997, there were only a handful of venture capital firms in Washington, most notably the Baltimore- and Menlo Park, California–based New Enterprise Associates. Two years later, there were dozens of local venture firms and outside funds doing deals in Washington.

New venture funds and incubators that were supposed to nurture young companies were ways to measure the growth— and the craziness—of the time. While it used to be difficult to raise capital, now there was so much money chasing deals. Another barometer of how hot the subject of technology had become to the city was the comeback of one media entre-preneur.

From 1980 to 1992, Bill Regardie had run a successful mag-azine that focused on real estate and banking during its '80's heyday. It wasn't so successful, however, that it could withstand the early 1990s recession. The magazine folded, losing about half a million dollars. Regardie returned briefly in 1994 with an avant-garde, arty magazine with striking black and white pho-tography, but closed that after just a year. In September 1999, Regardie debuted a third magazine, *Regardie's Power,* that would center on high-tech in Washington. To launch the magazine, Regardie held a lavish party at Sam & Harry's in Tysons Corner, the suburban hub of technology in the region. Downtown friends of Regardie's who had never been to Tysons before mixed with the tech elite, politicians, and journalists. Many people were happy Regardie was back—his particular style of journalism smacked of opinion, partisanship, and controversy. He knew how to get attention, beginning with the cover of the first issue, a photograph of a Fabio lookalike flanked by his employees, two bikini-clad women who are members of a traveling band of women who wrestle in oil. The technology angle here was . . . the Fabio guy owned the domain name www.americaonline.com and was hoping AOL would pay him dearly for the rights.

When Regardie launched this time, one of his friends, Doug Poretz, an investor and public relations adviser to technology companies, was supportive but realistic. "The real issue is 'How long will this period last for technology?'" Poretz asked then.

Regardie's Power was funded 20 percent by Bill and his wife, Renay Regardie, and the rest by outside investors. One of Regardie's early stops for cash was, of course, the Capital Investors. Regardie presented to the group in March of 1999. The club decided as a whole not to invest in the magazine, although Regardie convinced several individuals to put up what he says was a total of $200,000. One of the members who invested said he considered that giving the money to Regardie was "insurance" that he'd see no negative press in the magazine. Regardie, however, says that while the issue was discussed that night, he thought of each of the Capital Investors as fair game.

In late 1999, Holidae Hayes faxed a cartoon to her friends and clients titled "Instant Wealth Disorder!" It revealed four tell-tale signs that you or your child may be afflicted by the problem, including finding business plans stashed by teachers in your daughter's homework and catching your son talking about new hot IPOs with his personal trainer. It was getting funny because it had become ridiculous.

She was starting to see some of the wealthiest change their personalities. Some were becoming unbelievably arrogant; others consumed by guilt about their success.

"You don't get a 'How Rich People Should Act' book," says Hayes. "Money is alcohol. It exacerbates what personality is already there."

Some of the tech rich began to talk about wealth as "our problem," that is, how to responsibly give away money and use it to grow their businesses. Later, the problem for many would be simply how to hang on to it. But for now, the requests filled up the voicemail boxes and email queues of all the Capital Investors. A million here, a million there, an introduction. Charities were trying to understand these people—did they like art? Would they support the symphony? Most of the members' motives for philanthropy were similar to the wealthy of other ages. Some had causes they genuinely wanted to help. Others clearly wanted to spruce up their image, have their name on a building, or ensure a legacy. And there was some guilt that came from making a fortune at an early age.

There was also a growing chasm, known as the "digital divide," that separated not only the new rich from the long-time poor, but the Internet users from those who didn't own a computer. For some of the group, those who were geeks when they were growing up, it was strange to have so much attention showered on them. "It used to be I'd say I was in computers at a party and people would move to the other side of the room," says Capital Investor Gary Greenfield, who studied engineering. Now they sidled up to him to ask about his fascinating life.

Just before Raul Fernandez's company, Proxicom, went public in 1999, his chief financial officer received a call from another Raul Fernandez, a local jeweler. It seems the other Raul felt that because he had the same name, he should get a stake in the IPO's "friends and family" shares, those that are usually reserved for people who have helped the company in its early days. Proxicom's Fernandez laughed and said sure; the jeweler said he'd give the CEO a good deal if he came into the shop.

But as Proxicom's stock price plummeted, strangers were no longer so enamored of Fernandez. He was screamed at in Blockbuster while renting videos. Another irate shareholder, a fortyish woman, recognized Fernandez at a black-tie benefit one evening and began yelling about the sinking stock price, punching him repeatedly in the shoulder. Fernandez grabbed his wife and left. Proxicom's 2001 annual shareholder meeting was attended by armed guards.

There were four waves of layoffs at Proxicom, and hundreds of people lost their jobs. Fernandez says the first one's the hardest, and you have to resist promising it's the last because it probably isn't. After the first one, he says he started getting numb to it. He had to cut off limbs, one at a time.

Part of the problem was that he'd hired people at exorbitant salaries with huge perks, people he'd outbid competitors to catch. "We had a bunch of high-priced players not performing," he says. "Take a rapper and a sports player and put them together. That's what we had in this industry."

Fernandez began writing down what he calls "lessons." Lesson one is that he was right to sell Proxicom stock regularly, all along the way. Many didn't, or started too late. Some CEOs worried that employees and shareholders would see selling off as a sign of uncertainty in the stock. But many financial advisers said sell regularly, let analysts and anyone else who would care know ahead of time that you're doing it, and sell when you've said you will. Lesson two is when everyone, absolutely everyone, is getting into your business, you should know the clock is running out.

These lessons are logical in hindsight, but somewhere along the way, these tycoons lost sight of what they once knew to be true. Money on hand and customers on file were replaced by dreams and visions. When they look back now, they can't believe some of the decisions they made. It seemed as though it was a game where the person who spent the most money would win at the end. Now, says Art Marks, his "old/new" mantra is "Cash is more important than your mother."

But the craziness was continued through a food chain of entrepreneurs, venture capitalists, investment bankers, analysts, and the media. "We had a public venture capital market for the first time ever," says Ramsey, describing how Wall Street treated companies with no revenues like real IPO candidates.

It was simultaneously exhilarating and exhausting. "We're all just running so fast, I would love a day to be home," said Bill Melton at the height of it all. In the two previous weeks he'd been to Switzerland twice, Brussels, London, Paris, Tokyo, and Pebble Beach. It's all the same, he said, the hotels, the conference halls. "Four walls is four walls."

In January of 2000, CNN aired a segment showing a "snapshot of life at the start of the twenty-first century, an era of high-tech and high stress." The piece followed Capital Investor Jonathan Silver and his wife, Melissa Moss, who had started her own Internet company, struggling with their severely overscheduled daily life. Moss's business, Women's Consumer Network, eventually shut down.

But the problems went beyond the blinders-on, overworked mentality. People made huge mistakes. They spent money they didn't have. Those who wanted to change the rest of the world using business practices forgot some of the tenets of running a good company.

"It sickens me to walk through our London office and see the two-story fish tanks," says Fernandez. "What the hell were we thinking?"

CHAPTER FIVE

RESTAURANT NORA, WASHINGTON, D.C.

February 2001

IN THE BACK LEFT-HAND CORNER of a small dark room of Nora's in Dupont Circle, Jack McDonnell is having an animated discussion on his cell phone. His ruddy Irish face changes from desperation to excitement to worry to anticipation. He's running on the adrenaline of trying to close the biggest deal of his career.

He's here a bit early tonight and is trying to save his baby— a company he created called Transaction Network Services— from going down with its current parent company in one of the biggest disasters in the Internet's short history.

There's a meeting scheduled tomorrow where he hopes to find out whether he has outbid two competitors who also want to spirit the company away from PSINet, one of the original companies that connected people and businesses to the Internet. PSINet, while once one of the brightest stars in Internet business, is on the verge of bankruptcy, having landed in a pile of debt after making a string of expensive acquisitions. The company's founder, William Schrader, lost his own stock in the company after putting it up as collateral for a loan. McDonnell sold TNS to PSINet in 1999 and thought that chapter of his life was over when he saw PSINet pass over his chosen successors and install an outsider in his old office.

"I'm not ready to retire," McDonnell says as he sips a scotch. "Getting my old company back would be manna from heaven." PSINet sent out fifty "books," putting the company up for sale, seven potential investors bid and now three are still in competition. McDonnell says if he gets it, he'll sign on for two years to turn the company around. Sure, he feels sorry for Schrader, whom he considers a real technologist in a sea of pretenders putting up Web sites, but everyone's out for himself. "Sometimes the pioneers are the ones with the arrows in their backs," he says.

McDonnell is living in Florida most of the time these days, but says he's antsy. He found an investor who helped him raise the $285 million they're offering for the company. Quite a nice little deal, considering just a few years before, McDonnell sold TNS to PSINet for $780 million.

Pressure is also on tonight as McDonnell has brought the first investment deal he has sponsored to the Capital Investors, a portable cardiology device. Sponsorship has become political among the members. Those who bring a company to the group feel slighted if the group turns it down. Some of the proposals don't even make it past Sachs. He says he has turned down three of Greenfield's suggestions without even showing them to the group.

McDonnell has already put in $800,000 of his own money. "I'd like it sanity-checked by the group even if they don't invest," he says.

But the first presenter tonight is one of Saylor's protégés, Anjali Kataria, founder and CEO of RIVA Commerce. Her company uses software to simplify what's known as the "supply chain" process in the wine industry and help meet regulatory requirements. It's an unglamorous task, organizing inventory and smoothing the ordering system. But if it works, it saves money. Saylor stands up to introduce her, just as everyone takes his cocktail and seat at the long table with a view of a wine cellar and tapestries that line the walls.

"Anjali is an eclectic girl," Saylor says about Kataria, who is not yet in the room.

"Have you dated her?" asks Warner.

"I'm not invested in her or the company," responds Saylor in a matter-of-fact manner. But he is a member of her advisory board, a group she created to plumb for advice.

Kataria, a twenty-nine-year-old Indian woman with long black hair and a cherry red suit, walks in, strides to the front of the group, and begins talking confidently about how she has developed software that helps wineries more easily comply with government regulations. She has signed Mondavi and others as customers already.

"You're a lot better looking than Michael Saylor said you were," blurts McDonnell. There's an uncomfortable silence, which Fahey breaks by saying, "When you're looking for money you'll put up with anything."

But Kataria is not deterred. "Thank you," she says with a huge smile. And she launches into details about her experience and customers.

The red and white wine is flowing at the table as a backdrop to her talk, as the members dip bread in olive oil and read their handouts.

"Most advisory boards are namesake but I am very persistent in asking them to do real work," says Kataria.

"She is," agrees Saylor.

The door to the main dining room opens as appetizers are brought in, and her voice is drowned out for a moment by the clinking clamor of the restaurant.

Burton, Warner, and Gorog question her about software systems. Kataria uses one of the wines they're drinking to illustrate the path of her software. She says there are fifty-three regulations the wine-maker must deal with before he can sell the product.

"If they adopted what you're saying, will they be able to make more wine?" asks Burton.

It's not clear whether she intends eventually to market the

software to other industries. They seem to like her better than her idea.

"So, do you need to get beyond the wine industry to be successful?" asks Fahey.

"No. Well. Depending on what you mean by successful," responds Kataria.

"I'm curious, how did you choose the wine business?" asks Mandl.

"I've always wanted a vineyard," she says.

"I've got one in King George," says Warner quietly about his farm in southern Virginia.

"And I love regulations," adds Kataria, who dropped out of law school to start this business.

"Talk to the governor there," laughs Mandl.

As the discussion turns to ASP, ERP, SAP, Fahey looks dismayed. "I'm at such a disadvantage because I don't know what any of the acronyms mean," he says.

Warner gives the high sign to Sachs to wrap up Act One.

"We'd love to close our seed round with your support," says Kataria. The door opens again and dinner—leg of lamb roast with rosemary jus, pan-seared rockfish in a root vegetable chowder, and wild mushroom risotto—is brought in. Everybody claps and Kataria is ushered out into the noise of the main dining room.

"We do see a lot of smart people," says Kimsey.

"I'm in," says McDonnell. "She's quick. Anyone who can talk that fast . . ."

But not everyone is impressed. "It's too small," says Fernandez. "I just don't see a business."

"Ooh. Kiss of death," says Fahey.

Warner turns to Spoon. "Come on Alan, be positive."

"It's small," agrees Spoon.

As one of the newer members, Fernandez is trying to figure out exactly what constitutes a Capital Investors company. "This is in the fun category," Fernandez says. But he's clearly not used to investing just for fun.

"You might not make a ton of money but you might make some," says Kimsey.

"This has a chance if it gets bought out," adds Burton.

"Is there any other upside to this? Free wine tours?" asks Warner.

Gorog looks frustrated. He says the group has mistakenly fallen into a mind-set that if it's not a huge deal it's not worth doing. "We should remember one of our purposes is to nurture young companies and young people," says Gorog.

"She might even be a female executive rather than a girl by then," jokes Ramsey, in reaction to Saylor's introduction.

Mandl is still considering the business model. He says if Andersen Consulting decides one day to go into this business and puts five people on it, RIVA's gone. The group is weighing the decision, struggling with its own mission.

"The charter of this group is not to make money," says Singh. There are quick laughs all around.

"We've been pretty good at that so far," says Burton.

Singh suggests investing a small amount, $100,000, because she's smart. "We could help her in a significant way with an insignificant amount of money," Singh says. Warner says because of her customers, they should do a couple hundred thousand. Burton leans into Warner and says he knows he has a vineyard only to be able to write it off as a farm.

"Let's go to two," says Mandl, moving it along.

Sachs calls for a decision.

"Why don't we give her $150,000 and have her write a white paper on a *real* business?" says Ramsey. He says she won't get venture-backed on this model.

Kimsey says at some point someone will probably take a close look at how well the group has done as high-profile investors. That's something to consider.

"So we're in agreement? $150,000?" asks Sachs.

Now it's McDonnell's turn to introduce a candidate for investment.

"The hardest thing to do in the god-damn world is to be an after-dinner speaker to you guys," he says.

The company is LifeLinkMD, which has developed a distribution system to sell Automated External Defibrillators—machines that can jump-start a heart in cardiac arrest. These devices are portable, and LifeLink's vision includes making them as ubiquitous as fire extinguishers in public places, from hotels to airplanes to shopping malls.

McDonnell met LifeLink's founder and CEO, Dr. James D'Orta, in the emergency room of Georgetown Hospital when his son was in a car accident. McDonnell points out that the Capital Investors, all male, mostly in their forties and fifties, living a fast-paced life, are the kind of people who could eventually need these.

"All you guys are candidates for this box," says McDonnell, as they polish off pieces of apple-walnut pie and chocolate soufflé cake.

Kimsey tells McDonnell to speak for himself. But he has their attention.

Burton asks Kimsey if he has one on his private plane. "No," says Kimsey. "I'm afraid I'll pass out from wine and they'll put the paddles on me."

McDonnell clearly has an audience, right now, right here, in this room for this. He says anywhere there is high stress, there should be one of these. Mandl and Singh are interested.

Silver, looking at the handout, laughs as he realizes the presenter lives across the street from him in Georgetown, and he had no idea he was coming tonight. Three men in dark suits walk in.

They pass the machine around the table like a party gift everyone wants to see. The Capital Investors push the buttons, comment about its weight, and turn it upside down and around, looking at it very seriously.

"Is there a freshness time?" asks Fernandez about battery life and how long the pads work. About three years.

The presenter talks about deaths at airports and all kinds of other public places that could be avoided.

As they leave the room, Warner asks for a vote.

"This one saves lives," says Singh. Gorog suggests investing $200,000.

"But there's no technology here," complains Burton.

The discussion turns to whether members of the group would get free or wholesale defibrillators if they invest.

Ramsey starts talking about his announcement today that he's launching a combination hedge fund–private equity fund to invest in troubled companies. Most of the group already know about the "vulture fund" and several, including Warner and Sidgmore, have put their own money into the pool.

Out at the bar at Nora's, D'Orta is drinking port. "It's like waiting for the white smoke," he says.

The group decides to invest $200,000. On his way out, Kimsey grabs D'Orta by the ear. "Say this word after me," says Kimsey. "Oversubscribed." D'Orta doesn't know the word, but understands that Kimsey means he wants to invest and wants him to tell others that there's no more room for private investment, which would dilute original investors' ownership. His message comes across.

CHAPTER SIX

THE CRASH

EARLY PLANNERS OF ONE OF Washington's glitziest and most successful charity events were so enamored of their new technology donors that they considered renaming it the "Dot-Com Ball" in 2000. But the name didn't stick. That was just as well, because tech fortunes were falling and anything with "dot-com" in the title was beginning to seem a bit tarnished. Instead the decidedly less flashy "Best Buddies Ball: Friendships Through Technology" brought together the top techies with movie and sports stars for a great cause.

Still, many who arrived in early October for the twelfth annual ball, this year held at the Potomac home of Sargent and Eunice Kennedy Shriver, think of it as the Dot-Com Ball. That's because guests were greeted that chilly autumn evening at the Shriver's door by Michael Saylor and Raul Fernandez, who co-chaired the event with actor Kevin Spacey.

The evening was sponsored by Proxicom, MicroStrategy, and America Online, and honored Ted Leonsis and his wife, Lynn, who were huge donors of Best Buddies. It was considered Saylor's coming-out party, after months spent holed up working through an accounting restatement, a government lawsuit, and a downward spiraling stock price. There were other technology companies on the donor list that night that were struggling. It was beginning to be apparent that in technology philanthropy, share prices may not match up to good intentions. And a lesson to charities: Get it in cash, not stock.

Best Buddies was an A-list event with enormous tents out back and entertainment by Kool and the Gang and the Cirque du Soleil. Guests included Helen Hunt and model Angie Everhart, as well as the community's top venture capitalists and technologists.

Fernandez's table was the best in the house: He had Muhammad Ali, who had been honored a previous year, and sports owner Abe Pollin, considered the grandfather of Washington sports. The sports empire Leonsis and Fernandez are building, Lincoln Holdings, is a subtle nod to "Abe." Ball-goers flocked to the table to have their pictures taken with Ali, and praise was lavished on all the tech philanthropists.

They may have lost money, been beaten down . . . but on this evening they were the kings of Washington society. They were mainstream, no longer on the fringes. That night, they were merry. But the bottom was nowhere near.

In April of 2000, Fernandez had watched his stake in Proxicom cut in half, from a high of $898.4 million. It would again be sliced in two.

Fernandez said he'd been regularly selling off to avoid losing it all. "You don't count on it until it's in the bank," he said. "Paper worth is very overrated. If you really watched this you'd go nuts."

For most, it all began—or ended, really, depending on how you look at it—that March and April. As Ramsey puts it, "The unknown became known." Many of these technology companies weren't real. They would never have profits. And those that were real would be taken down with them.

"The jig is up," said Marc Andreessen, who was trying to create a new company, Loudcloud, that depended deeply on Internet business customers. "In a complete meltdown you learn a lot more," he added optimistically.

It hit John Sidgmore how screwed up everything had become when he learned that people at the lowest levels of WorldCom, including secretaries, were losing everything on margin calls. Then, Sidgmore's archrival, Bill Schrader, founder of PSINet, was stripped of every share he held in his company—he'd put up the stock as a loan guarantee. It was horrible. But that normal, everyday people were betting money they didn't have gave Sidgmore the creeps.

"The difference between $20 million and $100 million in your life is not that different," he said as this was happening. "The difference between $20 million and zero is big."

The so-called margin calls were disastrous. People were betting money they didn't really have in hopes of winning more money that didn't really exist. But others were seeing not only their personal finances erased but real companies they built crashing down.

"The tone was, 'Hi, join the parade,'" said Fernandez. "Now it's not."

Alex Mandl was having one of the toughest times of any of the Capital Investors. Mandl had joined Teligent, then known by the generic name Associated Communications, as chief executive officer in 1996, shocking Wall Street and the telecom industry. To run the unknown start-up, Mandl left the No. 2 job at AT&T, where he was president, chief operating officer, and heir apparent to CEO. Mandl's switch was met with much fanfare because he was one of the first high-profile "stable" economy leaders to leave the relative safety of his job for the unknown risk of a fledgling firm. When he joined, Mandl was given a $15-million signing bonus and would eventually hold options for six million shares of Teligent stock.

The company grew larger, developed technology, and began to sell it, all the while being watched closely, in great part because of Mandl's history. Teligent would sell voice and high-speed Internet access to businesses, competing with the regional Bell companies by using microwave technology antennas to receive and send signals. It attracted $1.8 billion in investments. But the company had fallen deep into debt by the time the crash hit. In late 2000, Teligent laid off about 780 employees; 200 more were let go in early 2001.

Teligent's market value of $6.2 billion in March 2000 plum-

meted to less than $50 million. Its stock, once $100 a share, sank
to below a dollar.

It fell upon Mandl's shoulders to raise money to save the
company. It was what became known as the "financing question." If you had it answered, meaning you had the investment,
Wall Street could be at least placated.

But the money was never raised. In May of 2001, Teligent
filed for bankruptcy, Chapter 11.

Mandl blames his directors. "My board turned down what I
wanted to buy and what I wanted to do," says Mandl. "They
rejected $700 million of clean financing. That was nuts."

Teligent had become adept at spending large amounts of
money buying spectrum licenses and building a physical network. Mandl was following the rules of the moment: Get big
fast. Worry about everything else later. Mandl gave up much of
what he knew to be true to follow what he thought the time was
dictating. In hindsight, says Mandl, he should have taken his
foot off the accelerator a bit in exchange for quicker profitability.

"A year ago, it was how much revenue can you generate,
almost at any cost. How quickly can you establish new markets,
how many buildings can you have, and how fast are you going?"
he lamented shortly before leaving the company. "At what mar-
gins or what cost simply was not part of the agenda. It wasn't a
factor. Today the world is very different. Today the world is
reflective of real business economics, real viable business models that reflect the basic principle of how do you make money,

how do you get a return? The capitalistic system was centered around how you invest money and make a return on that."

So how did Mandl, one of the most experienced business leaders in the group, forget those things?

"The pendulum over-swings in both directions," he says. "Things were valued in a way that was just totally absurd, frankly. And then it swings the other way and all of a sudden, the cold reality sets in of more basic business economics, and then everybody runs for the door."

Some executives got rich off their companies before they crumbled. Mandl did not. He says he and his wife, Susan, with whom he runs ASM (for Alex and Susan Mandl) Investments, are still living a comfortable lifestyle, but they have to be more conservative in personal spending habits after seeing their net worth statements disintegrate. Mandl never cashed in a single share of his Teligent options. "On paper, I lost a half a billion," he says calmly.

Spending on their collection of eighteenth-century art is a first casualty, he says. The Mandls are a study in opposites. Alex, a native of Austria, is gentlemanly, reserved, typically of few words. Susan, a former opera singer, loves to sing and dance, and talk loudly and passionately. Over the past few years, says Mandl, there wasn't a whole lot of time for vacations or hobbies. There might be more time these days. "He has created a lot of wealth and lost it at least on paper now," says Singh. "Will he be able to re-create it?" Singh, a long-time Teligent boardmember and one of the company's largest shareholders, says it's impossible to tell.

Mandl is trying not to second-guess himself. "Almost everything you do, you can wake up the next day and say, 'Well, what could I have done differently here?'"

Singh says two things went wrong with Teligent: It didn't raise enough money and it didn't spend the money it had wisely. "I think what happened is everybody caught euphoria and lost some of the discipline."

It's the spring of 2001, six months after the Best Buddies Ball and one full year after the tech crash, and the market has only grown worse. Even the mood in the Caps box this April evening has become less festive. "We are all shell-shocked," says investment banker George Stamas as he watches the Capitals play against the New Jersey Devils. Shrimp, fruit, and cheese are spread out on a large round table that overlooks the ice. Michael Jordan walks in, dressed in a dark pin-striped suit. He sits next to Leonsis in the front row of the box, his knees touching the Plexiglas in front of him. During a break he goes over to the bar and hugs the woman serving drinks.

Fernandez reappears after a visit to the team doctor, trying to find out what's wrong with his knee. "Now I just need a haircut, it's one-stop shopping," he jokes. Later that night, Leonsis and Fernandez will have dinner with Jordan at the Caucus Room restaurant downtown. Stamas, owner Dick Patrick, and Jordan's manager Curtis Polk would also be on hand for the first serious discussion about the star returning to the basketball court for the Washington Wizards.

"That night he said 'I want to play again,'" says Fernandez, who claims the owners were surprised, and of course, thrilled. "We never, ever thought in our wildest dreams he'd suit up."

But for now, Fernandez is thinking Proxicom, trying to woo a Fidelity portfolio fund manager who has invested in the company and is sitting in on the game. People are talking about MicroStrategy, PSINet, Ariba. It's all bad news, all around.

"This was our '80s," says Fernandez, unusually glum. Even the Caps aren't playing well, losing to the New Jersey Devils. "They're like our industry tonight," says Fernandez, glancing out over the ice.

In Washington, the result of building a successful community where everyone did business with everyone else had a devastating ripple effect.

The Capital Investors were expecting everything they touched to turn to gold. Instead, much of it was disappearing into ashes, with several of their portfolio companies running out of money with no end in sight.

Some members of the group were obviously focused more on their own company's survival. But those who were beyond that stage were embarrassed, and outraged that their bets weren't paying off. They were supposed to be the smartest group of technologists and financiers in Washington. Several of the group are professional venture capitalists. They could invest in almost any start-up. If they couldn't handpick winners, who could?

Their timing was off.

But it certainly wasn't just their list going under. Many other companies, including some of the ones they turned down, were going out of business, and venture capital funds, including ones managed by Capital Investors during their day jobs, were writing off enormous investments in failed companies. Susan DeFife's company, WomenCONNECT.com, which the group turned down but Burton and Warner funded privately, lost 90 percent of its value in two or three weeks. "On April 14, the rules changed overnight," says DeFife, who went on to become CEO of another start-up. Investors who measured a company's success by how many people looked at a site were now painfully aware that "eyeballs" didn't translate to cash. "It went from eyeballs to profits," says DeFife.

It became a time of second-guessing, wealth depletion, and canceled vacations. People talked about survivors rather than stars.

"The go-go days are over," sighs Doug Humphrey, who had founded Digex, a successful Internet service provider, in the early 1990s and was trying to take his new company, a satellite delivery service called Cidera, public. "All of a sudden, the future is farther away than it seemed," says Humphrey, whose company was funded by New Enterprise Associates among many other top-tier VCs.

David Levine gave his employees what he calls the "Winnebago speech." Don't spend what you have, certainly not what you think you have based on stock options, he warned. Don't splurge on that Winnebago yet.

"The sense was that you could solve the problems later," remembers Levine, whose company was funded by Capital Investor Steve Walker. "It was an emperor-has-no-clothes moment."

Executives who watched their companies' stock soar to ridiculous heights saw it fall lower than a dollar. Former hotshot firms like Varsity Group, which sells college textbooks online and was an early investment of Russ Ramsey's company's venture fund, were de-listed from the stock market. Waves of employee layoffs led to a disenfranchised technology workforce.

The same venture capital firms that were the cornerstones of new success suddenly had struggling investments, as if a disease were eating through their portfolio.

Many entrepreneurs learned they were naïve to think their venture capitalists would protect them. Somewhere along the way, company executives forgot that "attracting outside financing" means selling a chunk of the business, sometimes a controlling interest.

"It's pretty black and white in VC," says Suzanne King of New Enterprise Associates, who is on the board of Capital Investors portfolio company Cyveillance, talking about her own goal to make partner at NEA. "If you make money for the firm, you make money for the firm. It's pretty clear whether you're successful or not."

The VCs would replace the founder if they thought it would be better for the company. They would shut down the business if they thought it was burning too much cash. This is called, simply, "pulling the plug." Most venture capitalists have a pure goal of making money, which they then return to their own investors, and anyone who forgot that was reminded, rather harshly. VCs spent the spring and summer of 2001 doing triage, deciding which companies should live and which should die. They pulled the plug on some to put money in others that had a chance. Community building gave way to survival planning.

Art Marks of New Enterprise Associates shut down at least one company while it still had money in the bank. "I've seen this movie before," says Marks. "I don't want to wait until the end."

Marks says, "1999 and 2000 were very unusual. People got into bad habits. They were undisciplined as venture capitalists and sloppy as entrepreneurs."

Some venture firms decided to hold off raising money for a new fund; a few even gave back money that had already been promised. Venture firms raise their money from wealthy individuals, corporations, pension funds, and universities, among other sources. These funders loved the payouts of the late 1990s, but it was clear those kinds of returns weren't going to happen again soon. Incubators went out of business. And the companies that had built themselves on the backs of the dot-coms, such as Web designers and marketing consultants, weren't getting paid. That is, if they demanded cash in the first place instead of equity. The ones who thought it was smart to barter services for stock were left with useless certificates. The networking groups began to fall apart. Anyone with that much free time was either not working enough to save his company or was looking for a new job. Or both. It was all starting to unravel.

Even the golden boy Fernandez was having a bad time, glued to CNBC in a hotel room in Cancun watching Proxicom's value sliced and diced. Eight of his friends had taken him to Mexico for a last hurrah before his June wedding. "This is not the way I pictured my bachelor's party," he said. "Thank God there's a lot of tequila."

Still, in the midst of the gloom came a huge coup. When AOL bought Time Warner—not the other way around, said its supporters gleefully—the company transcended technology into the larger realm of media. For the group, it was a crowning achievement for the best-known member, Steve Case. But the financial rewards and individual connections did not only accrue to Case. Kimsey and Leonsis were still large shareholders. Melton was a former board member of AOL and National Geographic's Fahey was a former CEO and chairman of the Time-Life subsidiary of Time Warner.

But the AOL–Time Warner deal was less a triumph of technology than of old-fashioned selling. The merger was first and foremost about the future potential of advertising across all media. When tickets to Madonna's "Drowned World" tour, her first in years, proved almost impossible to find, AOL offered them to people willing to subscribe to AOL for a few months. They got that benefit through Madonna's music label, owned by Time Warner. And in August of 2001, the company announced the formation of a new advertising unit that would promote across the brands.

It was evident, already, in AOL service pop-up ads touting *Time* magazine or Business 2.0. The range of properties, including the rights to Warner Bros. cartoon characters like Bugs Bunny, to CNN, and to *MAD* magazine and *Time* magazine, would offer unprecedented, coordinated exposure.

But only if they managed it all correctly.

"The true lesson is that we're no different than traditional media," says Leonsis. "Most of the dot-com companies had one revenue stream."

After the merger, Leonsis assumed three major duties at AOL. He's supposed to find new sources of business, like AOL by phone. He also spearheads AOL's plans against and with Microsoft. But the largest job is personally pitching to 100 big clients—from pharmaceutical to auto manufacturers—how AOL Time Warner can deliver this across-the-media super-campaign. But can Leonsis master the carnival of so-called synergy? "Let us show you how we open a movie and we blow it through everything," Leonsis tells a potential client, a large fast-food chain. "What if we do this with your product?" "Blowing it out" as Leon-

The table is set, the entrepreneurs who will present their business plans wait outside, and the Capital Investors enjoy their first cocktail before a dinner club meeting at Citronelle in Georgetown.

At a Capital Investors dinner at Citronelle, just before the Virginia governor's race really heats up, Mark Warner asks his friends for donations one more time and thanks them for their support. Seated from left to right are Russ Ramsey, Art Marks, Jonathan Silver, and Jack McDonnell. Individuals in the group gave a total of more than $1 million to Warner's campaign.

In the fall of 1998, at the height of the Internet frenzy, AOL co-founder Jim Kimsey and his then-girlfriend, financial advisor Holidae Hayes, held a Great Gatsby costume party at F. Scott's in Georgetown. They are here with friends celebrating Kimsey's sixtieth birthday that evening. The invitation read: "It was an age of miracles, it was an age of art, it was an age of excess, it was an age of satire."

Laura Neuman, president of MaTRICS, presents her company's business plan to the Capital Investors. The group decided to invest $250,000 in the company.

In 1996, MicroStrategy chief executive Michael Saylor, pictured in his Vienna office, was named Washington's high-tech entrepreneur of the year. In one single day in March of 2000, Saylor lost $6 billion when the stock of MicroStrategy, the data mining company he co-founded, crashed. The market was reacting to an accounting restatement admitting the company had actually lost money over the previous two years when it had previously claimed to have made money.

Capital Investors chairman Russ Ramsey walks out of a group dinner in Georgetown carrying a bottle of wine, a parting gift sent by one of the portfolio CEOs. Ramsey, who co-founded investment bank Friedman, Billings, Ramsey Group, Inc., had recently launched a hedge fund/private equity fund that would capitalize on struggling technology companies.

Steve Case is chairman of AOL Time Warner, which is now struggling to merge its vast properties, ranging from CNN to MAD magazine.

Holidae Hayes, a financial analyst with wealth management firm Alliance Bernstein in Washington, advises half a dozen of the Capital Investors on their personal investments. She is a former counsel to the Senate Banking Committee and a Federal Reserve law enforcement attorney.

One reason the Capital Investors invested in Reggie Aggarwal's company, Cvent, an online event-planning company, was that Aggarwal is as good at networking as they are. Aggarwal first created the Indian CEO High Tech Council, which became one of the region's hottest networking groups. He was forced to lay off more than half his Cvent staff to survive the economic downturn.

WorldCom CEO John Sidgmore talks with Steve Walker at a Capital Investors meeting. When the Internet backbone company he ran, UUNet, merged with WorldCom, Sidgmore took a top role at the company, but spends much of his time advising start-ups. After being rocked by an accounting fraud scandal in 2002, WoldCom filed for the largest bankruptcy in U.S. history.

Alex Mandl shocked many in the telecommunications world by giving up the No. 2 spot at AT&T to lead a then unknown start-up, Teligent. Mandl left the struggling Teligent in 2001. Having never sold a share of his company's stock, Mandl estimates he lost about half a billion dollars, on paper.

David Holtzman, co-founder of Opion, which developed software to measure "buzz" on the Internet, tells the Capital Investors he needs more money. The group had invested $300,000 in the company. Holtzman shut down Opion soon after.

AOL co-founder Jim Kimsey and his friend, real estate-investor Joe Robert—self-styled missionaries of capitalism—exchange worldviews in Havana with Cuban leader Fidel Castro.

On January 19, 2000, the day Michael Jordan is named part owner of the Washington Wizards basketball team, he celebrates in the owners' box with new partners Ted Leonsis and Abe Pollin as well as President Bill Clinton. Jordan would start playing for the team the following year.

AOL executive Ted Leonsis met Raul Fernandez (left) when Fernandez tapped his shoulder one day from the row behind on an airplane, overhearing him talking about the Web. Leonsis hired Fernandez's company, Proxicom, to create an early version of AOL.com. Later, Leonsis brought Fernandez into his sports empire, and the two are owners of the Washington Capitals, and part-owners of the Washington Wizards, Washington Mystics, MCI Center, US Airways Arena, and Ticketmaster/Citysearch Washington.

Andrew Sachs, twenty-seven, is the president of Capital Investors, although he says it's silly to call anyone under thirty president of anything. He screens two hundred business plans each month, chooses the companies that present to the group, does due diligence on investments, and manages the fund. "It's like herding cats," he says of running the twenty-six-member group.

sis likes to call the process, involves databases, email lists, magazines, television, and the Web. Movies were the first test cases. The fast-food chain, Burger King, which has 12 million daily customers, did sign for a multimillion, multiyear deal with AOL.

By the summer of 2001, Case had become less visible at the company, appearing publicly only when he felt like it, which meant infrequently. He hadn't been to a Capital Investors dinner in months, though he continued to invest and speak individually with his friends in the group. Those close to him said he was aware of the arrogant reputation many of his technology compatriots were gaining and wanted to stay out of the limelight. Case even stopped writing those monthly letters to AOL subscribers in January of 2001, just as the deal closed. "He never wanted to be Bill Gates," said an AOL employee. It was clear his longtime No. 2, Bob Pittman—who replaced the unfortunate Razzouk—was more involved in the corporation's daily business. But Case was working on another project. Like many of his Capital Investor colleagues, he was concentrating on legacy— how AOL would fare historically, and how he, Steve Case, would be remembered.

"Someday when I'm an old man, somebody's going to ask me: 'What did you do during the Great Internet Boom?'" Case became fond of saying in speeches in 1998. He was still working on that answer.

In May 2001, Case spoke at the CNN World Report dinner in Washington, a gala event honoring international reporters of the cable news channel now owned by AOL. It still seemed strange that Case, who rarely liked talking to reporters and was famous for his preference of emailing answers rather than talking in person or on the phone, had become the chairman of this journalistic enterprise. But here he was sitting next to Ted Turner at one of the tables with the huge clear globes as centerpieces, laughing as the two seemed to share a joke, and then answering questions from CNN journalists afterward.

The CNN reporters were wondering about their own future. "Is this the last World Report conference?" one asked Case. "They don't tell me much now that I'm chairman," he joked. "This next phase is going to be very complicated. The lines are starting to blur." The questioner continued: "Is that a yes?" but did not get an answer.

"If the last decade of the twentieth century was about the Internet, then the first decade of the twenty-first century will surely be about convergence—as lines between traditional industries and media blur," Case told the crowd. Yeah, they'd heard that before. But the sheer number of important media properties now under their roof could change the game. Many reporters, however, feared what convergence—in their eyes, favoritism—could do to journalism. And business experts knew that combining the two companies with their diverse products and cultures—not to mention the egos of a slew of top executives would be one of the most challenging mergers ever.

When the deal was announced at the beginning of 2000, it was worth an estimated $183 billion. As the stock prices of both AOL and Time Warner fell over the year, the closing price ended up at $112 billion. There was no provision for stopping the deal if AOL stock sank below a certain price.

Certainly, as everything else was unraveling, the fact that Case and his crew pulled off the AOL–Time Warner deal at all was amazing. Looking back on it just a year later, it was AOL's salvation.

"It happened in the nick of time," says Sidgmore. "It wouldn't have happened now."

At a Capital Investors social event at Warner's Alexandria home, the members drank more than usual and alternated between serious philosophical discussions and crazy antics. Case ended up raiding Warner's closet that night, putting on some of his clothes and playfully jumping into Warner's bed.

Ramsey and Kim, who had sold his company Yurie Systems to Lucent for $1 billion, talked that evening about whether it was all worth it. "Why are you still working so hard?" Ramsey asked Kim, who was traveling nonstop for Lucent, working longer hours, and seeing his family less than when he was a start-up entrepreneur. "I still think we can catch Cisco," Kim said. "But after that I want to do something honorable, like teaching."

It was getting vicious. A labor shortage that had turned into a bounty hunter–style search, with employees given huge signing bonuses, stock options, and bizarre perks, turned into an era of layoffs and messy non-compete agreements.

Many of the group met up the next month at NEA's annual holiday party, a huge bash held at the Marks's Potomac house. The tech elite was out, bedecked in red and green and drinking eggnog. Children were everywhere, and there was really only one topic, though it came in many forms: the fall of PSINet and other companies, the press coverage, the dearth of venture capital, the pink slips, the market. There was a Santa Claus, but there was also someone dressed up as the Grinch, perhaps more appropriate for the mood. Ramsey, Sidgmore, Walker, and Warner were there. Saylor, dressed in a brown suede jacket, talked about his recent viewing of the American Presidents exhibit at a downtown museum. He complained absentmindedly about *The Washington Post*'s over-coverage of the new panda bears. You would never see that kind of coverage of grizzly bears, he said.

Warner had been going to a series of "birthday parties"— fund-raisers disguised to celebrate the day he turned forty-six. "I'm on a treadmill," he said. "I'm exhausted." He made the rounds nonetheless.

Only Walker seemed genuinely relaxed and happy. He pulled from his pocket a photo of his third and newest helicopter and showed it proudly to anyone who would look.

The ripple effect was continuing, not just in mood but in business. When a company canceled a local order, both companies lost money. "Our whole technology community is falling apart," lamented venture capitalist Rick Rickertsen of Thayer Capital. "It breaks my heart when I read the newspaper."

However, one person's misfortune is another's opportunity. Two of the Capital Investors who made the most of the worst times were Jack McDonnell and Russ Ramsey.

Ramsey had become a multimillionaire in the tech boom as co-founder and president of investment bank Friedman, Billings, Ramsey Group, Inc. Ramsey formed FBR with partners Emanuel "Manny" Friedman and Eric Billings in 1989 when the three walked out of another brokerage house to start their own firm. Early on, the firm focused on bank and thrift companies, then went after technology businesses in full force. FBR wanted to take tech companies "from cradle to AOL," acting as the early venture capitalist and public offering underwriter. But getting a hot tech firm to choose FBR over Goldman Sachs or Morgan Stanley for a prized spot on the front of a prospectus would be a huge challenge.

So FBR set about promoting itself as the hometown bank and Ramsey as the personal link to the community. He bragged that he'd never even been to the Valley. If Ramsey supported a local technologist, they'd become friends and choose FBR, right? It was part of the plan to build a community in which everyone helped one another. Some bought into that, but not always.

But others saw FBR as too regional. New York firms had

international ties and more connections outside of Washington. FBR also tried to cash in on the online investing craze, creating fbr.com, which was launched with television and print ads, designed to "democratize" the investing process. But FBR's underwriting business dried up and its own stock dropped to $3 a share.

While this was happening, the venture capital arm of FBR, created in 1998, was becoming the most profitable part of the business. The first fund of FBR Technology Venture Partners had blockbusters like webMethods, which had the third most successful IPO in history and at its peak traded at around $300 a share. The venture group rented space in the hip Morino building and its partners were popular fixtures in Washington's technology community. The second fund did not do well. And start-ups in every niche of information technology were falling apart. Not having another fund could be deadly—in the venture world if you're not raising money, you're dead. And in fact, that's what was happening to funds all over. They wouldn't file for bankruptcy; they would just quietly put many of their port- folio companies out of their misery and never go out to raise another pool of money again. In 2001, the two founding part- ners of FBRTVP suddenly left the firm.

Ramsey had become more interested in the venture capital part of FBR. For a brief while, it had been making more money and garnering more attention than the rest of the business. But Ramsey saw the slowdown the same way he had looked at the

Internet revolution in the early 1990s. It was an opportunity, and he could smell it. "My net worth went up in 2000," Ramsey says. He made money on the crash, and he was proud of it.

In February of 2001, Ramsey announced he was leaving his namesake company to start something new. It would be a fund called Capital Crossover Partners, which would make debt and equity investments in what it considered "undervalued" (read: dying) public technology companies. It would also make investments in private companies nearing the public markets. CCP is part hedge fund and part private equity fund, carefully designed to invest in struggling and successful companies at precisely the right moment, and then get rid of the investments at other right moments. It's built on the premise that throughout an economic crash, companies with real business worth are abandoned and can be snapped up at bargain prices. Sometimes just a database is worth saving, or a patent. These funds are often called "vulture" capital funds because they swoop in and pick through the refuse no one else seems to want. Ramsey doesn't mind being known as a vulture capitalist, as long as it means he's making money. But he prefers the term "opportunity fund."

"I like to look at busted Internet companies because no one's doing it," he says. Ramsey says he lives by his role model Warren Buffett's two rules: Don't lose money. And don't forget rule No. 1.

Ramsey had been considering leaving FBR since 1998 and was becoming an expert in "near-death-experience" companies through his family's personal investments. The harder it became for companies to recover, the better deals they became for him. "They have permanent scars," he says of his rehabilitation candidates. The crash, now, was on Ramsey's side.

On Sunday, the day before the announcement, Ramsey gathered a few of his employees to finish crafting the press release that would go out. They met on the eleventh floor of the huge building FBR occupies, in Ramsey's glass-windowed corner office that overlooks the Potomac River and the skyline of Washington. That floor would be the new headquarters for CCP.

"We've obviously had a circumstance where Nasdaq has crashed, we've had the technology bubble burst and a tremendous shakeout in venture capital for private companies," said Ramsey that day. "The investment opportunity that has emerged from that is substantial."

He smiled when he said, "The volatility is my friend."

At about the same time, a prospectus had gone out to potential investors in CCP. It wasn't the best moment to ask for money. This type of fund, too, was unfamiliar to many, and Washington had very few hedge funds at all. Capital Investor John Sidgmore signed up immediately, saying this hybrid fund was "relevant right this minute." Warner, Case, Leonsis, and Kim also invested. "He hustles," says Leonsis of Ramsey. "He's been more right than he's been wrong." Others stayed away—some had overextended themselves already with promises to other venture funds and charities as their stock price crumbled away. But by the fall of 2001, Ramsey had a $250-million fund, of which he personally had put up $10 million, and was making investments. Typical investments, or buyouts, would be in the $10-million to $15-million range, though CCP could make deals in the $50-million to $100-million range as the fund raised more money.

One company he looked at was Teligent, formerly run by fellow Capital Investor Mandl, whose property backs onto Ramsey's in Great Falls. Singh, too, was a director and major investor.

"You start with a big mess and you work it down," says Ramsey.

John "Jack" McDonnell decided not to invest in CCP, in part because he was pursuing his own project: buying back the company he'd founded in 1990 and sold to PSINet in 1999. McDonnell is an exuberant, talkative, scotch-in-hand Irishman. There is absolutely nothing politically correct about him. He is an Irish Archie Bunker with a penchant for jokes. ("Why did God make alcohol? To keep the Irish from taking over the world!")

Transaction Network Services sounds entirely unglamorous, but the Reston company has become a necessary part of our lives, creating software that makes credit card transactions go through by linking the credit card machines in retail stores to computers of card issuers. And it was a profitable part of PSINet, which otherwise was bleeding cash.

McDonnell, co-founder, chairman, and CEO of TNS, sold the company to PSINet in 1999 for $785 million in cash and stock. McDonnell personally made $15 million in cash and $15 million in stock on the sale. Soon after the deal was done, McDonnell attended an executive retreat in Charlottesville, Virginia. He says he drove away that day thinking the company was being run by madmen. A few weeks later, when McDonnell received his PSINet stock, he sold it all the next day.

For the next few years, McDonnell watched PSINet go on an acquisition spree and become one of the most important players in Internet business. In 1999, PSINet paid an estimated $100 million to put its name on the Baltimore Ravens' football stadium, a marketing ploy that confused many residents in Baltimore who had never heard of the company and didn't know how to pronounce "Pee-Ess-Eye-Net." Some began calling it "Pissy-Net."

As CEO of arch-competitor UUNet, Sidgmore offered, several times, to buy PSINet, but was always rebuffed by Schrader. Although his wealth and early vision of the Internet marketplace would have suggested Schrader might make a good member of the Capital Investors, he was never invited to join. He easily may have turned down the group if he had. People called Schrader the "Internet cowboy," and he rode alone.

McDonnell says the best thing to happen to TNS during its ownership by PSINet is that the parent company completely ignored it.

In 2001, as he watched PSINet fall apart, McDonnell began to cast about for investors who would help him buy back the company. It was about more than the money he'd make: McDonnell was bored and wanted a new challenge; he hadn't meant to retire. And he wanted back what he'd created. And who knew what would happen if PSINet went bankrupt? TNS could disappear. Clearly, PSINet needed the money, too.

A private equity investment firm based in Chicago, GTCR Golder Rauner, came forward with the best offer, putting $177 million into the pot. Six executives, including McDonnell, ponied up $8 million and the rest came from a loan from a group led by Deutsche Bank. McDonnell and his group needed a meeting place in which to plot the takeover. So McDonnell called Morino and the "Samurai Six," as the group was dubbed, began gathering in a small office at 11600 Sunrise.

Investment bank Goldman Sachs drew up an offering memorandum for TNS which was distributed to fifty potential buyers. The two final bids came from McDonnell and GTCR and Warburg Pincus, a New York–based private equity firm.

In April 2001, McDonnell and GTCR purchased TNS for $285 million. "We got the car back with a couple of dents," says McDonnell.

It was a family affair, with McDonnell installing his son, John J. McDonnell III, and his two sons-in-law as top executives. There was a lot to celebrate that summer at young

McDonnell's wedding in Ireland, attended by Capital Investors Fernandez and Gorog.

In the meantime, McDonnell's friend Bill Melton was watching his own baby blow up. CyberCash was one of the original Internet IPOs and a company many thought would change the way people bought and sold goods. While CyberCash was one of the first, it wouldn't last. Melton wrote a bittersweet letter to CyberCash employees explaining his resignation from the board of directors.

McDonnell figures he's one of very few people to make any money from CyberCash. He pulled his entire stake—$4 million—out of the company six months after its initial public offering. "They were ahead of their time," he says.

Ramsey and McDonnell weren't the only ones to seize on trying times.

In fact, the way law firms, public relations firms, and other companies came out of the woodwork during the heyday to serve successful businesses, a new breed sprouted up around the dying ones. One such adviser to struggling companies was Dot-Trauma.com, founded by Wendy Haig, daughter-in-law of Alexander Haig, former secretary of state.

All around the Capital Investors' table, people were shrinking from billionaires to mere multimillionaires. "I've lost another $100 million today," Kimsey would say as he watched AOL stock plummet.

Strangely enough, as venture capital firms struggled to raise new money in 2001 and did triage on current investments, angel money was again in great demand. During the height of the Internet rush many companies had entirely skipped the angel stage and went straight to the big pockets of venture firms. Now they were looking for seed money anywhere they could, especially if it came attached to some helpful connections. One of the reasons why the Capital Investors did investments in the first place—they saw a hole in the funding process that could slow down the success of the region—was once again relevant.

The good news for the Capital Investors, as well as any other private investor in 2001, was that they could get a much better "valuation" than before. In other words, they could buy a larger chunk of a company for less money. Some venture capitalists began using terms like *on sale* and *bargain basement.* Others set up the legal documents of an investment, known as a *term sheet,* with demands they wouldn't have thought of asking for a few years earlier. And some switched terms on a company at the final hour, knowing how desperate companies were to get any money at all. The companies in the worst shape were forced to do *down rounds,* meaning they had to lower their valuation for a second or third round of funding. It was going backward, but at least it wasn't going out of business.

Over at the Morino building, the camaraderie is still there, but the work-hard, play-hard mentality seems out of date now that people are being laid off, let alone having their designer water supply curtailed. The days of free beer and foosball are over.

Several tenants have gone out of business. Venture capitalists a year or two ago could be heard in the hallways whooping about a stock hitting $300 a share, but those corridors are quieter now. There is less champagne-popping and more scanning financials and recruiting new management.

And by June of 2001, the anchor tenant, Proxicom, was preparing to move out of 11600 Sunrise. "I don't want to leave the building," says Fernandez. "But I'm not the boss anymore."

It had hit Fernandez the previous summer that the company he had founded with $40,000 he'd saved as a down payment for a house could be in trouble if he didn't sell it or buy another company. The realization came to him right about the time he got married in Georgetown, in a Catholic ceremony with hundreds of flowers, followed by a lavish bash at the Four Seasons where Tony Bennett sang and guests received silver boxes with their own last initials engraved on the top. Among those circling the caviar and martini bars were Redskins owner Dan Snyder and arch-rival Jerry Greenberg, the CEO of Sapient. Holidae Hayes was there in a shimmery iridescent dress, as were Capital Investors Russ Ramsey, Mario Morino, Ted Leonsis, and Michael Saylor, whom Fernandez's cousin had brought as her date.

As Fernandez set off for a honeymoon in the Greek isles with Jean-Marie, his new bride, it was a rare chance to think about something other than work.

By then, Fernandez had decided to try to go what he calls the "Steve Case route"—buying an old-economy-style company. That would take Proxicom to the next level, he figured. Fernandez hired investment bank Goldman Sachs to look into a merger or sale. But it wasn't so easy. One company Fernandez targeted was in Chicago. Fernandez walked in expecting to find a CEO who would see why the two companies were a perfect match. Instead, the executive yelled across the table at him, "This industry is full of young guys with brass balls who think they can buy us." They didn't make a deal.

That summer, Fernandez worked on a merger in which Proxicom would combine with Aether Systems, a Maryland wireless company that had great success and then was hit hard by the meltdown. "It would have been a disaster," says Fernandez.

But time was running out. Still, Fernandez admits it was difficult to see at the time, in the midst of it all, what was going to happen.

"People were blinded by the idea that it was going to last forever," he says. "I was, too."

Lesson three: Watch those "fixed" costs, the ones that reappear on a bill every month or quarter, whether you've done well or not. Proxicom's biggest fixed-cost problem became real estate, which the company bought and rented as if growth would never end. Fernandez figures Proxicom lost about $30 million in fees for broken leases by over-estimating real estate needs.

It got worse through the winter as Proxicom's value continued to drop and the right deal proved elusive. Then, one of the investment bankers from Proxicom's secondary offering, who was working on a deal with computer maker Compaq, suggested Proxicom might be a good takeover target. At about the same time, Fernandez read in *Red Herring* magazine about a South African company called Dimension Data that was looking to buy a Web services company. The story listed several possibilities, including Proxicom. Fernandez says he'd never heard of Dimension Data, known as DiData in shorthand. But soon the South African company came calling, too. Talks with both Compaq and Dimension Data began in earnest in February, as the stock steadily drifted downward.

"Timing was always an issue," says Fernandez. "Every month that goes by it gets rougher and rougher."

And the potential buyers knew that as well. The longer they could stall, the better the price they could get for Proxicom. Compaq slowed down negotiations and watched the stock go lower. Fernandez continued to negotiate both deals, with each of the bidders being told there was one other in the game. They used code names on faxes and emails. DiData was "Denver" and Compaq was "Houston." Proxicom was code-named "Pacific" in the DiData negotiations and "Phoenix" with Compaq. DiData was the first to give Proxicom a term sheet. Fernandez called Compaq to let its negotiators know a bid from another company had come in. Compaq quickly came back with its own offer in March and a press release was prepared to announce the deal. But Compaq stalled again just as DiData was pressing to finalize its own agreement. However, DiData had one big problem—the unused real estate—which it considered a $180-million liability and a deal-killer. DiData wanted to pay less.

Fernandez says DiData at this point thought he was bluffing about the other bidder to drive the sale higher and force an offer. But then the Compaq board met, approving the deal and bringing its name out into the open. Proxicom officially announced that Compaq was buying it in April for $336 million. Fernandez did media interviews and embarked on a road show to tell his employees about the acquisition.

That Saturday night, Fernandez and his wife Jean-Marie, who left her job with a cosmetics company when they married, went to the Sting concert and then Cafe Milano in Georgetown with friends to celebrate.

Sunday morning, Fernandez, hungover from the festivities, received a call from DiData's banker. He said: "I'm going to make your life hell but you'll be a lot richer."

Fernandez shouted to his wife: "We got a higher bid!" This deal would be worth $448 million. Fernandez liked that. "It was a serious sign of love on their part," he says.

That day Raul and Jean-Marie traveled to Charlottesville, Virginia, meeting both their families to celebrate her father's birthday. Fernandez was on the phone the entire time. The next day, he went to London as planned to talk to Proxicom employees there about the Compaq deal. Fernandez spoke with Compaq's CEO, expecting a counteroffer. To his great surprise, Compaq didn't come back with another bid. "I felt helpless," says Fernandez. "I couldn't control it." There was no way to not take the higher price.

Fernandez continued on the European trip, talking to employees in London, Paris, and Munich about the Compaq deal, with a growing sense that he was pumping up the wrong suitor. On a conference call in Lisbon with DiData, the company began asking Fernandez why he lost certain deals, focusing on Audi. Fernandez was exhausted. He broke down and yelled at them that the deal was off unless they had no changes to the term sheet already offered. "It wasn't hostile but it wasn't not hostile," he says of the takeover.

DiData said fine. Proxicom prepared to pay a $10-million "breakup" fee to Compaq. Fernandez's chief financial officer suggested sending the $10 million, all in pennies, in a fleet of armored cars to Compaq headquarters. Fernandez, still irked that Compaq hadn't stayed in the game, considered it.

On May 18, just days later, Fernandez went out again on the same road show, this time to tell employees about a different acquirer. About 200 Proxicom workers gathered at the Reston Sheraton, grabbed a beer or some wine on the way in, and sat down to hear the second version of their company's takeover.

"Well, it feels like we were just here," laughed Fernandez, wearing gray pants, a lavender long-sleeved shirt, and a BlackBerry clipped to his belt. "And we were."

Fernandez made his speech and the déjà vu road show moves on to New York, Chicago, San Francisco, Los Angeles, and London, where he meets the same employees and tells a slightly different story.

"I'm tired," says Fernandez. "I'm happy."

A usual condition of a deal like this is the "non-compete," an agreement that at least the top executives will not go work for a competitor within a certain period of time. Fernandez says that was easy. As the deal was being crafted, many of his top people began studying . . . biotechnology. They thought the next big thing will be in the life sciences, and the Washington region, with Human Genome Sciences, Celera, and government resources like the National Institutes of Health, is positioned to be the center of that universe, too.

One of the strangest things about the post-crash time was that even the good technology companies in Washington were disappearing, many of them bought by outside companies. Network Solutions was bought by VeriSign, a California company; UUNet became part of Mississippi-based WorldCom. People worried that the AOL–Time Warner merger would move the big decision-making to New York.

It was hardly the best time to start a new company and nearly impossible to get out in the public markets. Still, in March of 2001, a moment when the concept of doing an initial public offering was a joke, one of the Capital Investors took his company public. Marc Andreessen, the group's Silicon Valley representative, had joined Capital Investors during his brief stint as AOL's chief technology officer, when he wanted to get to know the Washington tech crowd and consider some start-up investments. The six-foot-four Andreessen is intense but shy. He is one of the most technologically savvy of the group and shares other members' impatience and interest in digging deep into certain subjects. His friends say he is a perpetual student and obsessive reader. Andreessen, who had in his twenties famously co-founded Netscape, the company that arguably began the Internet business craze in the first place, took his new company, a Web services firm called Loudcloud, public that spring.

The cherubic face of Andreessen represented the good old days of great Internet innovation, and optimists looked to this IPO to jump-start the public markets. But Loudcloud opened at a disappointing $6 per share and continued to fall, hovering under $2 in August. Many of Loudcloud's investors were now "underwater," meaning their stakes were worth less than they had paid for them.

"That was nonsense," says Andreessen about the great expectations that Loudcloud could single-handedly stimulate the market again. The point was to raise some big cash, he says. "People forgot what IPOs are."

Also in March, investment adviser Holidae Hayes sent a calming email, with the subject line "market turbulence" to her high net worth clients as their piles of gold disappeared around them. This was a year after D-Day in technology stock history, April 2000, when things had started the slippery slide.

Hayes, who has worked as a law enforcement counsel for the Federal Reserve and as chief international counsel for the Senate Banking Committee, was now a principal with Alliance Bernstein in Washington, a large wealth management firm. Hayes devises investment programs for individuals, families, and foundations and gives her clients advice on charitable giving and inheritance planning. During the crash, she says, conservative investments are once again in vogue. "The investments aren't glamorous, just smart," says Hayes, a tall, beautiful woman with long copper-colored hair, a Kentucky drawl, and a tendency to snort when she laughs. "Leave the glamour for personal lives!"

Although Hayes does not talk specifically about her clients, she is well known as a personal adviser to many of the Capital Investors, including Bill Melton, Mario Morino, Raul Fernandez, Mark Warner, and still, Jim Kimsey. Many of the members also have the same personal lawyer, Stephen Comiskey, who has become a professional sports owner himself, buying a lacrosse team called Washington Power.

"Volatility creates opportunity," Hayes wrote. Then she pointed out to her clients that the boring old companies that had been ignored for the past few years were looking good. Consider utility companies, railroads, and paper companies, she said. It was not particularly what technology investors wanted to hear, and certainly not what those running the companies could even process.

But those who had avoided—or missed—the craziness were relieved. Those who never were part of the Internet euphoria began talking about how, thank god, things were back to good old normal.

One of those was John Fahey, CEO of National Geographic Society and a somewhat unlikely Capital Investor.

"I don't like people to think I'm a member of the group," he admitted. He doesn't get the acronyms at the meetings and he's not an owner of his company because that's not the way the non-profit Geographic Society is set up. Even with four magazines, a hundred books published a year, and expeditions around the world, there are no annual reports. Nationalgeographic.com brings in about one-half of 1 percent of the group's revenues, says Fahey. And they don't spend much money on it.

He gets a kick out of the group, he says, and the decision-making on investments that "depend on the phase of the moon." But he's aware that the arrogance of the Internet rich is grating on many. However, Fahey admits he was a bit jealous a while ago. Like many other established firms, National Geographic had considered a dot-com spin-off. "It's kind of a relief," he says, that that period is over.

"I feel a lot better on my perch than I did," he says now. "There was a great exuberance and everything was a bit surreal for a while."

By the end of the summer of 2001, the outlook was still bleak. AOL laid off hundreds of workers in August and Cooley Godward, one of the law firms that had beefed up to cater to the technology market, dismissed about 17 percent of its junior lawyers, an unusual move in the legal world.

And so many of the Capital Investors had mislaid their golden touch. But no change of fortune was as swift as the one who provoked not disillusionment but satisfaction and even glee in some quarters.

"It's like watching Donald Trump being beaten up," said April Young, a Washington banker. She was talking about Michael Saylor.

THE GEORGETOWN CLUB, WASHINGTON, D.C.

April 2001

MICHAEL SAYLOR, whose MicroStrategy stock is hovering at about $2 a share, down from a high of $333, laid off about one-third of his staff a week ago and is not here tonight. It's one of the first dinners he's ever missed. Also absent is Alex Mandl, whose Teligent is veering toward bankruptcy. And Jeong Kim who is trying to steer his division of Lucent to a more profitable path. And Raul Fernandez and John Sidgmore, who are also managing unhappy investors and employees.

As members sit down on red velvet chairs at a long table set with silver, china, and tall white candlesticks, with lit chandeliers lining the walls, Jim Kimsey looks around. He says that if a member misses three or four dinners, his business is clearly in trouble.

At the members-only Georgetown Club, men must wear coats and ties, or be forced to don an ill-fitting jacket that clubs like these keep on hand for those who forget the rule or don't comply.

As the Capital Investors gather in the antique-filled, formal cocktail room at the club, they compare ties. Several of the members laugh about how they had to go home to change first. For the Capital Investors, most of whom feel more comfortable in open shirts and casual pants, the dress code tonight matches the somberness of the technology industry.

There does not seem to be much good news. Warner looks exhausted from the campaign. Walker talks about how his new venture—a helicopter commuter service—has been thwarted by Virginia activists who don't want landing pads near their homes. Melton has just seen his baby, CyberCash, file for Chapter 11.

As the wine is poured, Ramsey asks out loud what's on everyone's mind—"So, what about the gloom and doom?"

"We should take a pool on when the market will come back and trade on that," says Melton.

Ramsey says he's seeing good things in non-start-up industries, such as automobiles.

"I'm scared because of what I read in the paper," says Greenfield. "It's scary to watch the other enterprise software providers go down. It's truly scary."

"What about having the biggest loss of wealth in history?" asks Kimsey, considering the meltdown of both real and paper profits generated from Internet companies. There is not much chatty banter tonight. They are not invincible.

As the spinach salad is served, Silver has a slightly optimistic thought to offer, saying that a box manufacturer he has invested in just had a record quarter.

"Consumers should be slowing at this point," says Ramsey. "Up until now they haven't."

Greenfield concurs. His wife is a real-estate agent—on the front lines of measuring consumer confidence. He says that her clients still give her increments of how much they'll go up above the list price to beat a competing bidder. Home-buyers are still bidding up, up, up. Everyone nods. When that's not happening, times have really changed.

"Let's all sell our houses quick and then buy them back next year," quips Warner.

"You have to finish building first, Jim," says Walker to Kimsey, who is designing a mansion in McLean, Virginia, Walker's Capitol Rising helicopter taxi service has flown Kimsey around his property to get an aerial look.

"It's a great bachelor pad," says Kimsey.

If residential real estate hasn't changed yet, commercial real estate has. Companies are pulling out of leases and leaving big chunks of office space on the market. Just a few months ago, it used to be one of the biggest challenges for a technology company to find any space at all in the over-glutted market.

"MicroStrategy had all that space it didn't fill and now it

never will," says Kimsey. Proxicom, too, found itself stuck with lots of useless real estate after several waves of layoffs.

Someone asks Morino whether his building, which houses technology companies, is in trouble, too. "We had a couple of companies go down," he says. "But that's not an anomaly." Some companies moved out because they got too big, also. And others moved in.

"So the answer is we don't know," says Melton. "I'm preparing for two to three years down. If it goes up before then, God bless me."

"You go to your financial advisers and say, 'Show me your Armageddon situation.' I did that," advises Warner.

"It's time to listen to them," says Walker.

Melton says he had lunch with Jeong Kim that day and he's remarkably bullish.

"But he took out a billion cash," says Warner.

"He sees things turning," says Melton. "On the other hand, if you bet and you're wrong, you're screwed."

"That's why instead of just doing private equity, Core is looking at doing a small hedge fund," says Silver. Others are thinking that way, too, with a growing number of "vulture" funds swooping in to make bargain investments in struggling companies. Ramsey set up his own version of a private equity–hedge fund in February.

Ramsey smiles. "Russ, will you stop smirking," says Warner.

Tonight the presentations are a bit different. There's only

one new company pitching, and then two companies the group has already invested in will give updates and ask for more money. So far, Capital Investors has not re-invested in any of its companies. But the members could decide to change that rule, or individuals could pony up.

Two executives from Viztec, a company that makes interactive smart cards, enter the room. They stand at one end of the long table and the group keeps talking. "Take it away," says Sachs. "Just start right in," adds Silver, who is sitting nearest to the presenters. The CEO, Jim Graham, looks at the group, most of whom are not looking at him. "Just start right in?" he asks Sachs.

Then he does, just as steaming plates of filet mignon with mashed potatoes and asparagus or Alaskan salmon with dill mousse are served to everyone except the two entrepreneurs.

"I'm absolutely convinced we have the elements of success here," says Graham. He talks about his experience as the knives and forks clink against the china and the members chew their meat.

They talk about their patents and pass around tiny cards with clear plastic displays.

Graham mentions two important meetings he's had recently, with financial firm Capital One and veteran smart-card company Gemplus.

It's not clear if he knows that Kimsey is on the board of directors at Cap One or that Melton knows Gemplus well from his years with CyberCash.

"Did Gemplus say no?" asks Melton. Graham says they're still talking about Gemplus signing on as a customer, but that there hasn't been a yes or no yet. "Did you meet with Marc? You need to get to Marc. He's the only one who sees over the hill," says Melton about Gemplus's chairman Marc Lassus.

"What's the voodoo in this?" asks Ramsey. "Obviously it's a logical application. What's the breakthrough here?"

"What's to keep someone else from doing this?" adds Walker.

As the fruit tarts come out, the discussion turns again to patents and Melton asks which law firm is representing the company.

Graham adds that although much of the company's development is ongoing at Kent State, he's moved the company to Washington and is looking at office space at 11600 Sunrise, the Morino building.

Sachs shuttles the two out as the group claps. Then he closes the door and walks back in.

"How much due diligence have you done on the patents?" asks Melton of Sachs.

Silver jumps in to say that Core Capital looked at this deal six or eight months ago, but passed. Silver thought it was an interesting technology, but was concerned that it was in early development and not yet ready for commercial use. He also didn't like that the new CEO wanted to stay in Washington while the company was really based in Ohio.

Melton is concerned that the CEO is wasting his time meeting with someone at Gemplus who doesn't make decisions.

"That's where we could be helpful," says Sachs.

"How good is the patent? We could turn around and sell this to Gemplus," says Melton.

Kimsey also thinks Capital One would be interested. "They have loads of money."

Warner is holding his head in his hands, looking tired.

"This is a lot more of a significant deal than we've seen in the past," says Silver.

Warner suggests Kimsey and Melton follow up with their contacts.

"Assuming the patents are any good and the tech is real, I am happy to call Marc at Gemplus," says Melton.

"And I want to put $50,000 into it," says Warner.

The mood has officially shifted.

Next up is FastTide, already the beneficiary of a $400,000 investment from the group.

Sachs mentions that Jeong Kim has personally put $4 million into FastTide.

Warner says his investment firm, Columbia Capital, invested in FastTide also.

"Unfortunately, I have some in this, too," says Melton with his arms crossed.

"I didn't do anything with them, did I?" asks Kimsey, sensing the sinking feeling around this company.

After this dubious introduction, the entrepreneurs walk in.

Ken Lee, a young man in a stylish dark suit with a slightly scared look on his face, stands at the end of the long table and addresses his investors.

"In general, the story may not have a happy ending," he says earnestly. "It will be very difficult to survive."

Lee explains how the company started as a Webcaster. That didn't work, so it was remade into a software business. When that didn't take off, FastTide became a hardware company. The investors are starting to laugh a bit. What have they gotten into?

Lee looks out across the table at his audience and delivers the blow. "We pretty much used up all the money at the moment," he says. "We can't get customers, we can't get VCs, we don't have any money."

He goes on to explain that in its latest incarnation, the company is a storage business. "I'm very negative on Internet, telecom, or anything."

"So are we," says Kimsey.

"If you had $5 million, what would you do with it now?" asks Silver.

Lee says that since last Thursday, he's been learning the computer language XML.

Ramsey asks how that plays into storage. Lee says, "Well, it doesn't."

The group is getting restless. This guy has lost their money and it doesn't seem he has any plan to get it back. His numerous attempts to re-create the company smack of desperation.

"If you could wave a magic wand and do anything, what would you want the company to be?" presses Silver. Lee says he'd like to run a router business.

As everyone quietly drinks coffee and the dregs of their wine, it's looking bleak.

"What have you got that no one else has got?" asks Kimsey. "What's the secret sauce?"

"He's got a storage company . . . till next week," scoffs Walker.

Kimsey says that at AOL, he had to change course, too. But he doesn't get what Lee is trying to sell. Silver suggests that Lee talk to another local XML company, webMethods, to see if it would be interested in acquiring Lee's technology.

"We have to build it first," says Lee.

Silver looks shocked. It's worse than he thought. There's nothing there to sell. "Not sure I knew that," says Silver, shaking his head.

It's clear the situation is dire, and the group isn't being of much help. "What can we do for you tonight?" asks Walker.

Lee looks relieved. This is what he's here for. He says he needs two things. One is help getting out of a lease in Tysons Corner, a 30,000-square-foot space that is costing him $80,000 a month. "The only way to get out of that lease is to file for bankruptcy," he says.

"It's Chapter 7 or Chapter 11, one way or the other," says Melton.

Walker asks what the other wish is. Lee says with a monthly burn rate of $200,000, he needs a $5-million investment.

As a storm rattles the windows, Walker says under his breath, "Note the thunder at that point."

Heavy rain and hail hit the building. Branches are flying off the trees outside, a violent end to a spring day when the temperature in Washington reached a record-breaking 91 degrees.

"You had faith in me. I'm doing the best I can," says Lee. "We'll do our best to get your money back. But the chance of that isn't very high. I'm hanging on to strings."

"An intelligent Chapter 11 could help you a lot," says Melton.

"Good luck," says Silver.

Lee leaves and the members look around at one another. If this was unusual, it would be no big deal. But it seems like too many companies in their portfolio are fading. Weren't they supposed to spot the next big thing?

Sachs says the next company set to present is actually doing well. The members look pleased. These guys don't like to lose. Greenfield says Sachs certainly had them in the right order, hoping to end the evening on a high note.

Reggie Aggarwal, a young Indian entrepreneur with a lock of dark hair falling across his forehead, stands in the spot Lee just left.

Aggarwal is a nonstop talker who created a technology council for Indian executives and then, quitting his corporate law job, launched a company based on the deep network he'd cultivated.

Cvent sells its event-planning service to companies and organizations that use it to invite people to conferences, parties, and other events through the Internet.

He begins with the obvious. "For the past six to twelve months, it's been humbling for all of us," he says.

Then he gives some good news. Over the last ninety days, Cvent has signed up more than one hundred new customers, including four of the big-five accounting firms, McDonald's and AOL Time Warner.

"Our space is humongous," he gushes, talking in Reggie-superlatives.

But then his mood turns, ever so slightly. Everything, after all, is not exactly perfect. Aggarwal says the one thing the company lacks is someone with real company-running experience. "But you're a schmoozer extraordinaire," says Warner.

Aggarwal introduces Marty Pinson, a tall, skinny, gray-haired man in a gray suit. Aggarwal says Pinson was once an executive at US Office Products, a company that went spectacularly bust.

"We have a real business here," says Pinson. He explains to the group that Cvent is trying to raise $9 million and they are here to ask the Capital Investors to participate.

Cvent is in a bit of a bind, actually, because a Pittsburgh venture capital fund, Birchmere Ventures, has agreed to invest $3 million in the company—but only if Cvent is able to raise $1 million from current investors. Birchmere wants to gauge past investors' faith in the company. Aggarwal stands in front of the Capital Investors tonight $180,000 short of that goal.

They are trying to save money, he says, with plans to cut their eighty-eight employees to the low sixties by the end of the month.

"How long have you been on board?" asks Melton.

"One week," says Pinson, laughing nervously.

Ramsey and Silver start grilling Pinson on contract values, burn rate, and which employees do what.

Aggarwal talks, and talks, and talks and talks.

"Reggie. You're giving me a lot of words," says an impatient Melton. "Cut the words. I've got a question and you're going to give me an answer." Melton wants Aggarwal to agree to sign a letter that would make the founders responsible to the investors for dilution of their investments. "We're getting washed down significantly because your current VCs are saying wash or else," says Melton. "I'm asking if the founders are willing to put their money where their mouth is."

Aggarwal starts into a convoluted explanation, and Melton interjects with, "Yes or no."

"No," says Pinson.

Ramsey continues questioning the sales quotas, contract recognition, accounting.

Looking at the numbers, it's becoming clear that Cvent isn't doing that great after all. Several members sigh.

"These are different meetings than we used to have," muses Walker.

"So, if we put up two hundred grand, you have some glimmer of hope, and if we don't, you're screwed?" asks Kimsey.

"If we don't close this in forty-eight hours we close the company," concurs Aggarwal.

He says he's been working on this deal for the past few weeks with Birchmere, but he hasn't been able to raise that last bit of money.

"Birchmere has the same attitude as all investors," says Melton. "It's take it or leave it or up yours."

Hearing himself talk, even Melton himself seems surprised at how negative he's become.

"I used to be a nice guy," he laughs.

"What's the risk-reward ratio on this? We're going to double our money and we get nothing?" asks Kimsey.

Ramsey interjects that Capital Investors has never done a follow-on round in any company. Doesn't look like this will be the first.

"This is more of a plea to individuals," explains Sachs.

Melton's had it. "You're the one sitting on the purse strings, Marty. Reggie, you're a great salesman. But this is no time for talk." He points at Pinson. "We're looking for you to tell us when you'll be cash-flow break-even."

"I'm ten minutes into this job," pleads Pinson.

"I'm forty-eight hours away from your close," retorts Melton.

Kimsey asks Pinson why he took this job in the first place. Pinson says this is what he does, he builds companies.

"But as an investor, I don't want to get washed out again," says Melton. "We're interested in some protection to a second bath."

"Then give us $5 million," says Pinson.

"In this market, are you kidding?" says Melton.

Sachs jumps in, saying it's time to cut off this presentation.

"Thanks for your time," says Aggarwal. But this is a problem no amount of connections can solve. Aggarwal appears shocked. What he does best is convince people to believe in him. Now his magic doesn't work.

As the Cvent team walks out, the members look distraught.

They're silent for a moment and then Greenfield says, incredulously, "It blew up on them."

Silver mentions another company he'd brought to the group that the Capital Investors turned down. They're doing great, he says, maybe he should bring them back for another shot. They could really use a winner now.

Most are still thinking about Aggarwal, finishing their mixed berry tarts. "And that was supposed to be the good news?" Kimsey asks Sachs.

"Well, compared to some of our other companies, that is good news," he replies.

Kimsey looks embarrassed. "We're so smart," he says, shaking his head.

"Money talks and bullshit walks," says Ramsey.

"Reggie *is* full of shit, isn't he?" asks Kimsey.

"Have we got any good companies?"

Sachs mentions one that's doing well at the moment, Core Communications. "Not to add more bad news, but at Webversa, we fired the CEO and laid off 75 percent of the staff. It's on life support right now."

"What doesn't kill you makes you stronger," offers Kimsey.

"Hmm. Good times," says Walker.

CHAPTER EIGHT

MICROTRAGEDY

ICHAEL SAYLOR IS TALKING about being humble. He is enunciating the word, breaking it into two parts. How important it is to be *hum-ble.*

He is still blaming others for the troubles MicroStrategy has seen, and he does so relentlessly this day, too, angrily telling anyone who interrupts the flow that any break in his train of thought irrevocably changes what he is saying. It wouldn't matter if there were 300 people in the room, or just Saylor, or, as there happens to be in reality, three people. The speech so often includes the word *humble* that it seems like a leitmotiv someone has advised him to include. He is sitting on a black leather couch in his Tysons Corner office wearing a black turtleneck, black corduroys, and a black leather jacket. A guitar signed by comedian Dana Carvey leans against the wall, inscribed to *Michael.com,* a Web address that MicroStrategy owns. On the coffee table, a book about skyscrapers makes an odd relic of mighty visions past.

Saylor feels that he is the persecuted one, the single technology executive made to shoulder the blame of the roaring Internet age. And in fact, some people believe that the day in March of 2000 when MicroStrategy announced that instead of posting profits for the past two years, it should have really announced losses, was the moment the crazy, unrealistic Internet bubble burst. It was as if Saylor had walked into a wild all-out party and all the revelers took one look at him and sobered up. From Saylor's point of view, however, his numbers people had messed up and what followed was "a witch-hunt for someone who did something wrong because if there was this much money lost somebody must have done something wrong."

In the space of two years, Saylor's hair has turned from dark brown to an ashy gray, as his company's stock price fell from a high of $333 per share to about $1. His face, always pale, has become chalky, and he has taken to wearing all black, head to toe. Perhaps he is wearing black because he is gloomy, but even more likely he's decided that one color is easier to maintain, one less thing in a multitude to think about. There are things that happen to a person whose fortune drops from $13 billion to $100 million. Saylor once lost $6 billion in a particularly bad single day, the one when he had to "restate" MicroStrategy's earnings. MicroStrategy stock dropped 62 percent that day, shaving $11 billion off its paper value. Lawsuits, including a government suit accusing fraud, followed. Just a week before, Saylor had pledged $100 million to start an online university.

"We think this is the wake-up call for investors that have

bought Internet-related companies," Jonathan Moody, a finan-cial analyst with Scott & Stringfellow in Richmond, told *The Washington Post* the day of MicroStrategy's restatement. "Maybe it calls into question how we value those stocks."

Saylor's company, once nicknamed "Master of the Uni-verse" after its stock symbol MSTR, is now called "Micro-Tragedy" by stockholders, the quintessential example of the Internet moguls' fall. It's not so fun being Michael.com after all. He's quite bitter about it. "The only thing you can count on is that if you make a technical mistake in this town there are peo-ple who will kick you to death in the head while you're on the ground," says Saylor.

At many Internet companies, the celebrity-status was dif-fused, shared among several executives. But to shareholders, the media, and the rest of the outside world, Saylor and Micro-Strategy were interchangeable. If one was succeeding, or dissolv-ing, so was the other. Saylor had always given the impression that he was the single person in charge, for better or, now, for worse.

So as the company fell apart and critics demonized the person in addition to the company. Saylor struck back at some, suing Yahoo chat-board posters calling themselves ursa_major_245 and lunchfeces, for defaming him. He is still as proud as ever but he does admit one thing about his strongest detractors: "I handed it to them on a silver platter."

When the world was looking for someone to blame for the arrogance and craziness of the Internet boom, Saylor and his company were the logical choice. He had gotten richer, on paper, than just about anyone, he was only thirty-five, he'd never run a publicly-traded business before, and he had a strange propensity to talk about himself and his company in historical terms. Over the years, he compared himself to Alexander the Great, Caesar, and even Mother Teresa—she never quit when things were bad, and neither would he. "Mother Teresa is simply an iconic figure that represents a person who is passionately pursuing her ideology," Saylor explained. "Fluctuations from each twelve-week period don't matter. If you're fixated on changing the world, it doesn't matter."

Marc Andreessen, who met Saylor through the Capital Investors, says he respects Saylor's intellect enormously but is glad he's in charge of a single company rather than something like the U.S. army where he could really do some damage. "He is a cross between Larry Ellison, Bill Gates, and Genghis Khan with a little bit of P. T. Barnum thrown in," says Andreessen. "Thank God he doesn't have his finger on the button."

Saylor was an army brat who grew up mostly in Ohio. He dreamed of being a pilot, but a heart murmur prevented that from happening. Instead, after graduating from the Massachusetts Institute of Technology, he worked on projects for Du Pont. Still in his twenties, he started his own data mining company, MicroStrategy, which he moved from Wilmington to Washington simply because he was impressed with the architecture of Union Station.

In the early days of MicroStrategy, Saylor surrounded himself with friends. MIT fraternity brother Sanju Bansal was the smiling, silent co-founder. Saylor was the one who would bang his fist on a table and talk nonstop except to ask a rhetorical "Right?" after he made certain points.

At first, Saylor's quirks seemed charming. He may not have let someone else get a word in, but at least he was talking about something big, about changing the world. He was not out for the easy Internet buck or early retirement. He didn't seem to know how to hold a fork, he brought his mother to events, and he had little patience for disloyalty, mistakes, inefficiency, thinking small. While other technology executives were building fast to sell quickly, Saylor talked about creating something that would stand through all time. He was particularly fascinated by a Spanish bridge called Alcantara. When asked what his favorite book was, he chose the eleven-book series on the history of civilization by Will and Ariel Durant.

People wanted to like him, understanding that brilliant people are often eccentric. But time after time he insulted them, said the wrong thing, spoke too loudly, until it didn't matter anymore how genius he was, if he was at all. Even his diehard fans were shocked to hear a comment he made at the 2001 annual shareholders meeting, in front of investors and reporters. He compared layoffs to "shooting dogs." He said the first one is hard, but by the eleventh one, it's part of the "natural life cycle." If employees didn't make the cut, he said, he would "close them."

Saylor based his company in Tysons Corner, in a building officially called Tycon Tower, but better known as "Tycoon Tower" or the "shopping bag building" because of its shape. He kept close control of the company, refusing to take any venture capital investment and appearing as the only "face" of the business. In the early years of MicroStrategy, Saylor lived in a town house ten minutes away in Vienna, Virginia, but he spent most of his time in the office.

To prepare for the company's initial public offering in 1998, Saylor often stayed up all night reading the prospectuses of some 250 companies that had already entered the public markets. The way he saw it, the one thing the companies he admired had in common was selling something greater than a mere product or service. Estée Lauder was selling beauty. Ralph Lauren was selling style.

An early motto of MicroStrategy was "a crystal ball in every desktop." The company had created software that would mine vast amounts of data and come up with strategic information. McDonald's could hire MicroStrategy to test how many more Filet-O-Fish sandwiches were sold in Chicago versus San Francisco. Victoria's Secret hired MicroStrategy to analyze the nation's bra-buying habits, sizes, and choices. But by the time MicroStrategy's own public offering prospectus was issued, there was a new slogan showing just how vital Saylor intended this company to become: "Information like water."

Investment banker Russ Ramsey met Saylor when he

solicited his business for MicroStrategy's initial public offering. Saylor had just fired one underwriter of the IPO, Goldman Sachs, because he didn't like the way its representatives acted toward him. "I will hire you if you don't treat me like a kid," Ramsey remembers Saylor telling him. Saylor says he did say something like that to try to cut through the formality between bankers and corporate executives. "Since this was my first IPO, I remember telling him that I expected the best possible service and that we expected to be treated as sophisticated customers, not naïve newcomers," says Saylor.

Ramsey was one of many in the technology community to befriend Saylor early on. Some wanted his business, others heard him evangelize about the world in his nonstop, free-flow of ideas, full of historical references and off-kilter analogies, and thought he could be the next Bill Gates, quirky and brilliant. Someone to bet on. Some also tried to pull Saylor into their social world, introducing him to single women and inviting him to cultural events. In January of 2000, Saylor joined Ramsey and about ten others on real-estate investor Joe Robert's yacht, where they sailed around the Caribbean, from St. Bart's to St. Maarten's and other islands for a week. Saylor became part of the Capital Investors, but more widely, part of the club in Washington.

While MicroStrategy's software was gathering customers and much positive recognition, it wasn't completely fulfilling Saylor's dream. He had developed another division of the company, Strategy.com, that would deliver instant news and information to consumers through a variety of wireless and wired devices. It was Saylor's vision, the way he would change how people communicate with one another. Saylor would demonstrate the service excitedly, showing how you could instantly find out that your mother's plane was late, or your child's school was closing early, or your stock had tanked. In the future, he said, bulletins would be more specific. If you were entering a mall where a robbery was taking place, it would tell you to leave. One of Saylor's favorite uses of the service was the "Dead CEO Alert" that would ping the investors of a company whose chief executive had wrapped himself around a tree. Would they like to sell, buy, or hold based on that information? While it seems like an exaggeration in anyone's words, Saylor said that Strategy.com would make the world a safer place. It would "purge ignorance from the planet," he promised.

"Our goal is to make Strategy.com the intelligent operating system," he said when announcing his plans. Saylor said that most newspapers would eventually offer the service over their site in an attempt to "monetize eyeballs," invoking two of the most-used jargon words of the time. What he meant was that newspapers were trying desperately to find a way to get the people looking at their sites to pay for the privilege. He would do deals with wireless companies. Saylor said he planned to invest about $100 million over two years in the effort.

"How is it we're going to commercialize this business?" Saylor asked of himself. "We'll get people's trust."

Trust and loyalty have always been important to Saylor. He created the company with an unusual quarterly program—each period had an event designed to improve morale and enmesh the worker with the company. Every summer, the entire company would go on a Caribbean cruise. Another quarter, each employee could fly family members to Washington for "friends and family day." He held an annual boot-camp training program to keep every employee updated on his job. And the holiday bash was huge. As good technology workers became harder to find, perks like these and the creation of a MicroStrategy company culture did much to attract new employees. The company thrived, and the stock soared to $333 per share. Saylor began preparing for a secondary offering and was concentrating more and more on his Strategy.com dream.

Saylor had hired a man named Mark Bisnow to be his chief of staff, a right-hand confidante who would advise Saylor in matters personal and professional.

As his title suggests, Bisnow has a political background, the height of which was a stint as John Anderson's press secretary in the 1980 presidential race. Bisnow, then in his twenties, became so well known for clearing an unusual path from the press to the candidate and his guileless answers that cartoonist Garry Trudeau featured Bisnow in "Doonesbury" as a running character throughout the campaign.

This time around, as technology became a new power in Washington, Bisnow was managing the Mike Saylor campaign in a similar way. Bisnow became wildly successful at making Saylor available and interesting to reporters. Saylor would always return calls and he would always have a great, if often bizarre, quote to offer. Bisnow helped his boss organize extravagant parties, like a Super Bowl bash at a rented-out stadium FedEx Field, the local football stadium, and an annual black-tie Oscars Party. Just before the Internet market crash and the company's own problems in early 2000, Bisnow had begun to push a bit harder, saying that while in the past the public wanted war heroes as its politicians, it would soon elect technology business leaders, because they were the ones changing the world. "We're looking at the last throes of a dinosaur class of politician," declared Bisnow, who added that these new candidates would have billions more than Steve Forbes. "I could easily see Mike running for president in eight or twelve years," he said then. And on Saylor's thirty-fifth birthday, his friends threw him an "old-enough-to-run-for-president" party at Cities restaurant in Adams Morgan.

Bisnow encouraged Saylor to keep a high profile, especially in *The Washington Post*'s Reliable Source, a widely-read daily gossip column that portrayed Saylor as a billionaire boy bachelor. In 2000, *People* magazine profiled Saylor as one of its 100 Most Eligible Bachelors, along with George Clooney and Ben Affleck. The goal had been reached—people knew who Michael Saylor was.

But then Saylor, encouraged by the media who expected

him to always give a colorful statement, and buoyed by interest and a rising stock price, began making what some thought were ridiculous comments. The historical references, at first intriguing, were grating after hearing the same ones over and over. It looked as if he had become a sort of king of MicroStrategy, without listening to any of the subjects. Sometimes it seemed he'd say anything that came into his head, and that was okay. More than okay for reporters. "The whole name of the game was get on CNBC, talk the vision," says Ramsey about high-tech public relations. People expected him to be interesting, and he lived up to that promise. At the same time, though, his tendency to run on for hours without letting someone else get a word in the repetition of his statements and his inability to ask for advice were wearing on people. Saylor had purposely conditioned people to think of him as eccentric. But there was a fine line between quirky and kooky.

Looking back on that time, says Saylor: "We lost control of our public image, first to our benefit and then to our detriment." Saylor looks at every story about him in the press as either having a "positive halo" or a "negative halo."

"We warned him to be careful," says Warner, who says Saylor went through a period where he wouldn't listen, said some stupid things, and thought people who weren't his friends were on his side.

"You've got to build friends," says Warner. "He didn't build his friend network first."

Some of those in the Capital Investors who watched Saylor become more and more unbearable decided to take him on as a project, to knock some sense into him and help him find his way. They had already started a Pygmalion-type process by encouraging Saylor's social life. It was now clear he needed some business lessons, too.

Warner tried to buck up Saylor by talking to the press about him, explaining that he had a real vision. Many of the group had worked on their images through some high-profile philanthropy, and they suggested Saylor do the same. But, true to form, Saylor would not be content merely to start a conventional project or donate to a museum.

At the 2000 *Washington Business Journal*'s annual philanthropy summit, the top gathering of its kind in the region, Saylor announced plans to use $100 million of his own money to create a nonprofit online university, where people from any city or town could take classes through the Internet from world-class professors. Others, including Michael Milken who created the for-profit UNext, have launched online universities.

It was, to say the least, an ambitious goal. Many applauded Saylor's sense, again, of wanting to do something big. He invoked historical figures, saying it would be invaluable to have been taught by Lincoln or Beethoven. But those with years of experience in philanthropy and education questioned the project. What about human interaction? And who was this guy, anyway? People were not quite sure he was for real.

Other speakers at the same summit have been Steve Case and Mario Morino, who had both become known as creative philanthropists in high-tech Washington.

"The comparison was striking," says Morino. "Steve comes across with class." Saylor, he says, did not. "He asked for it," says Morino about Saylor's fall.

It wouldn't be long. In fact it would have been difficult for Saylor to have made a more ill-timed announcement.

About a week later, Saylor was on the road pitching investors on a secondary offering which he hoped would raise $2 billion for the company. He got a call from his accountants at PricewaterhouseCoopers saying that MicroStrategy would have to issue a "restatement" of its earnings during 1998 and 1999. For the past two years—MicroStrategy's golden moments—the company had been losing, not making, money.

Saylor was stunned. The stock plummeted more than 60 percent the day the restatement was announced. On that single day, March 20, 2000, Saylor personally lost $6.2 billion in paper profits. The following day the *New York Post* ran a huge front-page picture of Saylor. The general public, especially those individuals who felt they had missed their chance at Internet riches, had found someone to blame. Stories about Madonna and the Pope the same day garnered only small pictures above Saylor's head. But this was hardly just bad press. The U.S. Securities and Exchange Commission then sued for fraud and furious investors also sued, arguing they were clearly misled.

"We got caught in a very wicked set of cross-drafts," says Saylor. "It's like some kid on a school ground who plays football and gets too much attention too quickly," says Saylor, his voice gradually becoming slower and quieter. "When he finally makes a mistake a lot of people take glee in the fact that he fell and broke his jaw. The only difference here is that they don't just take glee, they can actually help push you down farther and farther, until they're standing on your back."

Ramsey was skiing in Telluride that March week with his family when he woke up, poured some coffee, and went to read the news on his ski-house Bloomberg terminal. When he'd left Washington, he thought his work on MicroStrategy's secondary offering—Friedman, Billings, Ramsey Group was slated along with Goldman Sachs as underwriters of the deal—was done. "I thought I was still sleeping," Ramsey remembered, as he read the announcements of the restatements. "It's a great tragedy."

It turned out that a March article in *Forbes* magazine, questioning the company's accounting practices, had attracted some careful readers at Goldman Sachs, one of the other bankers on the secondary offering. They went to MicroStrategy's auditors, PricewaterhouseCoopers, and asked if there was any issue they should know about. "That was seven days before the entire thing blew to hell," remembers Saylor.

The sticking point is what is known as "sales recognition"—during what time period was a product or service actually sold. Since public companies are judged by Wall Street on "meeting their numbers" quarter by quarter, the timing of sales reports can drastically affect stock price.

According to Saylor, a local office of PWC had approved accounting for the revenues from certain contracts up front, rather than over the term of the agreements. But after a review, the national PWC office decided to overturn the decisions of their local office. "The reason for the restatement was that about $100 million of contracts were booked in one fashion with the full approval of the auditors and then they retroactively changed their mind," says Saylor. "Literally the debate was did it fall in period X or period Y?" Citing a policy that PricewaterhouseCoopers does not comment on client relationships, a spokesman for the firm declined to be interviewed on the subject.

It became clear that the future of MicroStrategy depended on how the accounting issue, followed by the shareholder lawsuits and SEC inquiries, was handled. Ideally for MicroStrategy, it could be swiftly overcome in a settlement—like AOL had done a few years before in a separate accounting case—and forgotten as quickly as it had come up. But it was also possible that these issues could haunt MicroStrategy and hurt it in the long run.

Ramsey said he immediately advised Saylor to get beyond the SEC investigation as quickly as possible to avoid any perception of illegal activity that could cause outsiders to distrust the company.

And Saylor agreed, well aware of the stakes at hand. "We can't afford to string out [the civil action] for seven years because as long as it's hanging over our heads no one wants to invest in the company," says Saylor. He said he knew that if he didn't settle, the SEC was likely to subpoena every customer and every employee of MicroStrategy. No one would want to invest in or work for the company. And customers would not count on a company that may not be able to fulfill its obligations.

Indeed, in April, MicroStrategy came within a few weeks of going bankrupt, says Saylor. The company's commercial bankers had pulled its credit lines.

While it worked well on the way up to bill Saylor's personality as a plus for company, it backfired on the way down. Suddenly the company cruise, once lauded as a great perk, was an embarrassing, expensive boondoggle. It was canceled. And so, more substantively, was the secondary offering.

The person who had said as long as he had a dime he'd never let a good employee go, laid off thousands of workers. And the guy who had talked incessantly about trust and about not cutting corners was the leader of a company that said it was making money when it was losing it. Saylor describes the experience in nightmarish terms. "It's like waking up with your arm handcuffed to the bed and a bear in the room and having to extract yourself from that," says Saylor about that time of his life.

While Saylor may not feel like he did anything wrong—he particularly blames reporters, accountants, and lawyers for the company's troubles—he did learn that not everything, even at the company he birthed, is in his control.

Saylor is furious at PricewaterhouseCoopers, saying that even though he runs the company, he holds the firm responsible. He says that as a first-time CEO, he did not understand the fine print and expected that the people who he hired to worry about it would take care of it. "If you retain an auditor you have the right, at least I believe you have the right, to expect them to take responsibility for accounting technicalities," said Saylor. "You pay them, right?"

"They misaccounted and they never fessed up, they never so much as said they're sorry, they just did it," says Saylor. "Why wouldn't I blame them? If you started a company and you trusted your auditors to help you manage this stuff and then the books blew up, and you found yourself being attacked left and right by every single person in the world, then [you have] your life taken apart while your auditor basically backed into a corner and scampered off to a vacation in Tahiti and took no responsibility, wouldn't you feel a bit mistreated?"

Saylor compares the situation to a car manufacturer who builds an auto, puts an engine made by another company in the car, and when the car blows up because of the engine, the manufacturer is blamed. "I managed to get myself responsible for all of this when in fact I'm the one who's least qualified to make those decisions. I didn't make any of them. All those decisions were made by auditors."

Regardless of who was to blame, it was clear the restatements were affecting the bottom line. In August of 2000, MicroStrategy laid off 234 employees, about 10 percent of its staff. In addition to the pink slip and the severance package, each worker received $10,000 in MicroStrategy stock from Saylor's own holdings. The month before, the company had to tell more than 200 new college graduates that jobs they had been offered were no longer available.

In October of 2000, MicroStrategy executives agreed to pay $10 million in stock as part of a shareholder lawsuit settlement. Then in December, Saylor and two other top executives at the company each agreed to pay SEC fines of $350,000 to settle the accounting fraud case. None of them admitted any wrongdoing. Although the penalties don't take a huge chunk out of Saylor's still-estimable fortune, the SEC said these were the largest fines ever levied in such a case.

If Saylor were just completely obnoxious or rude, he would be easier to understand. But he has friends—not just new ones who rode on his train on the way up, but ones who've known him since high school and college—who say really, he's just a guy who wants to make a difference. He's just got an awkward way of acting that's not socially acceptable. Julie Holdren, founder of software firm the Olympus Group, has known Saylor for years. Her husband and Saylor were fraternity brothers at the Massachusetts Institute of Technology. Holdren has done business deals with Saylor and gone to movies with him. She says he's brilliant and kind and incredibly misunderstood. Conventional people will never get Mike, she says. On the other side, however, are those who have written him off.

Morino has heard Saylor on the humility campaign these days, and he doesn't buy it. "Do you know what Golda Meir said?" asks Morino. "Don't be humble. You were never that great."

There were other falls among the Capital Investors, but Saylor's was the hardest. Saylor also learned how his friends in the club would support or ignore him. Some members publicly supported him, especially Russ Ramsey and John Sidgmore. On the other hand, Morino, Fernandez, and Gorog tended to distance themselves. "It's the price you pay for playing the role," says Fernandez about Saylor's misfortune.

Following the company's problems, Saylor still showed up to almost every Capital Investors dinner, the most vocal member.

Saylor says when the restatement occurred, the Washington technology community split in half, for him or against him. "The day before it happened, everybody loved me," he says. "And the day after . . ." It hit him how things had changed when a news story criticized him for rudely disappearing for ten minutes during a philanthropic event. He was in the bathroom. "Getting up and going to the bathroom if everybody loves you is a non-issue," Saylor says.

Art Marks emailed Saylor after the layoffs and told him they were the right thing to do. Marks and his wife Nancy Casey, who runs a hedge fund, had Saylor over for dinner at their Potomac home. They thought Saylor hadn't cut back enough. "He's suffered from his own youth and not enough guidance," says Marks. He says whatever you think about Saylor, he's being himself, which is rare in a world of polite networking and back-scratching. "I like him because he's unapologetically arrogant," says Marks.

Al Berkeley says he went over to see Saylor one day "to see if Nasdaq could do anything." "We make behind-the-scenes connections," Berkeley says, like introductions among business people. But there wasn't much he could do. Berkeley calls the MicroStrategy saga the "dark side of American success."

As MicroStrategy fell, many began comparing Saylor to Larry Ellison, Oracle's CEO, who is also known for saying what he thinks and not worrying about offending anyone in the way. Despite Ellison's personal peccadillos, he's considered by many to be a great leader. Saylor's supporters wanted to believe that while he too could be a pain to work with, he was also capable of great things.

Burton, who had gone through his own share of corporate ups and downs while CEO of software company Legent, says that channeled properly, MicroStrategy could be an Oracle. Oracle, too, went through tough times when some questioned whether the company could survive. "Ellison did it in spite of the odds," says Burton.

Morino says when he first met Saylor, he was so struck by

the combination of arrogance and brilliance that he looked at him and said, "You're the living reincarnation of Larry Ellison."

At each dinner, says Morino, everyone waits for Saylor to give at least one long speech. "He can grate on you," says Morino. "But you don't bet against him."

Some thought, however, that the Capital Investors didn't do Saylor any favors with their advice. "They fed the worst in Michael when he was young," says Esther Smith. "After he got involved with those guys he started breathing his own fumes."

Saylor lists the people who were supportive as if they are etched on a tablet somewhere. He has saved every note, remembers every phone call. Russ Ramsey raised millions. Joe Robert, Mark Ein, Jim Kimsey, Ted Leonsis. "I got nice notes from Ted and others saying 'You'll get through it, it'll make you a better businessman.'" Ein, a venture capitalist and also a single thirty-something Washingtonian, invited Saylor to parties and introduced him to a young crowd of socialites.

But the Capital Investor who came most substantively to Saylor's aid was John Sidgmore, of WorldCom, who had famously built UUNet into a world-class Internet company and brokered some of the most important deals of the Internet age along the way. Sidgmore and Saylor met each other as members of the group. They learned more about each other hearing the questions posed to entrepreneurs at the dinners. "He was an intriguing character," says Sidgmore. In February of 2000, Sidgmore joined the board of MicroStrategy, fascinated with the potential of the company's wireless Internet technology and its big-thinking leader. A scant three days later, there was a Sunday night emergency board meeting to talk about the accounting issue. "I was thinking, what did I get into?" says Sidgmore.

But instead of leaving the company, Sidgmore increased his role. In September of 2000, Saylor chose Sidgmore to replace him as chairman of Strategy.com, hoping that such a respected new leader would deflect some attention away from himself.

"This will not be 100 percent Michael Saylor," Sidgmore said the day he announced his chairmanship. "It will create a different image and additional outside credibility."

Sidgmore also has a guitar in his office, this one signed by all the band members of U2. But he has a stronger penchant for the 1960s—a lava lamp and posters of Woodstock and Jimi Hendrix dominate the walls. The nostalgic decorations compete for space with the ubiquitous white board, that white laminated version of a chalkboard that was the epicenter of every technologist's office, full of multi-colored circles, arrows, boxes, and lists of merger targets.

Sidgmore began concentrating on devising a sales plan at Strategy.com, which he called a "large start-up." Strategy.com gathered other technology leaders for the board, including former Network Solutions CEO Jim Rutt and Dave Oros, the CEO of Aether Systems. The board was trying to build a dream team of executives who could steer some of the attention from Saylor and show that there was more to the company than one person.

Sidgmore said he'd like to spin it off, but not until the market improved. He'd run it separately from the parent company until then. "He takes our advice now," Sidgmore said of Saylor a few months after taking the Strategy.com role.

"Now my name's on this so I'm going to make it work no matter what," Sidgmore said.

The other members approved of Sidgmore's coming to Saylor's aid, although several of them said privately that they worried Sidgmore was risking his reputation. "John will bring adult supervision, which is exactly what Michael needs," said Gorog. Still, Gorog thought Saylor was the one to be held accountable. "I blame Mike," he says of the company's troubles. "He's a brilliant technologist but he has very, very little experience from a business standpoint. . . . You can't run a public company by the seat of your pants."

Singh remembered tough times at LCC, when he had fired a CEO and the company was in trouble, and he got calls from people asking if LCC was going under. He liked getting those calls because it meant people were concerned and interested. "They're not saying that because they want anything from me, they say that because they empathize," said Singh. "Some of them have gone through the same sort of thing." So he called Saylor and told him to focus on work. "Whether you will succeed or not, it depends on what the business really is," Singh told Saylor. Still, whatever the business did, analysts and investors had difficulty separating the company from the person.

Throughout the restatement, the investigation, the layoffs, and the stock fall, Saylor went to almost every Capital Investors dinner. He brought several start-ups for the group to consider for investment. One was software firm RIVA Commerce, run by a young woman named Anjali Kataria. Saylor had met Kataria through Bansal, who had invited her to MicroStrategy's Oscar parties.

The morning she was to present to Capital Investors, Kataria practiced in front of Saylor at his office in Tysons Corner. He was not happy with her presentation, saying it was too complicated and didn't have crisp enough numbers. "He said I was overconfident and arrogant," says Kataria. They worked on it for an hour and a half. That night, the Capital Investors asked many of the same questions Saylor had prepped her on, and she was ready with the answers. The group decided to invest $200,000.

Kataria says it makes her furious that people project images on Saylor that aren't real. "I think it's hard for people to connect with him, but that's because they haven't made the effort," she says. "Some of the most profound people in our society are hard to reach out to."

She relates more to Saylor now that she has the responsibilities of a CEO. "You're alone," she says. "I never understood that before I started my own company."

But another company Saylor brought to the group, one he had already invested in, was turned down. Andrew Sachs remembers Saylor was not happy about the decision. "The group shot [the entrepreneur] down pretty quickly and Michael threw one at me across the table—'Andrew, I told you, just because I brought it to you doesn't mean you have to bring it in,' or something of that nature. So I think, thanks a lot. But it was fine. It was a good deal anyway. I've said no to a number of the members bringing in deals and I would say no to Michael Saylor," says Sachs.

Saylor says he's learned some things from this experience, but they are not what one might have expected a young businessman to have learned from leading his first company. They are more insights one might hear from a movie star who got famous too fast and now just wants to be left alone. He is particularly bitter about his public exposure.

"I come from a white Anglo-Saxon Protestant male middle-class engineering background," says Saylor. "I am just about as mainstream normal as you can get in American society. So to go from non-noticeable in any regard to the top of the hill where everything went through the roof to under the bus, all in a short period of time, was extraordinarily educational.

"At this point I find it much easier to sympathize with the downtrodden. I find it much easier to sympathize with the persecuted, to those who don't trust the police, to those who don't trust the government, to those who don't trust the press."

In March of 2001, Bisnow left. Then two of the other top marketing and public relations executives departed. Micro-

Strategy would later sue one of them for taking other employees with him. Bisnow landed at software company webMethods, which had one of the most spectacular initial public offerings ever but was plodding along now along with most of the other tech stocks. Bisnow said he wanted to do for webMethods CEO Phillip Merrick, a soft-spoken Australian, what he did for Saylor. Bisnow and Saylor rarely speak to each other now.

Anonymous posters to financial chat boards have struck upon MicroStrategy and Saylor, whom many tend to call "Mikey," as a favorite thread. Thousands of messages about the company have been posted on Yahoo message boards, and the conversation goes around the clock. One writer points out the coincidence that MicroStrategy's troubles started in March and Saylor has compared himself to Caesar ("Beware of the Ides of March").

During the summer of 2000, Saylor decided he should start spending time with people outside Washington, beyond the realm of technology. One evening he ended up at a party given in the Hamptons by Sean Combs, the rapper known as Puff Daddy, or more recently, P. Diddy, at which everyone wore all-white. Saylor loved that party, loved the idea that everyone dressed the same. So that fall, he had an all-black party, for which guests were told to dress completely in the darkest color. Saylor, who himself had recently traded in double-breasted suits for a uniform of all-black casual, figured more people would have black clothes than white in Washington. The party was at

Saylor's new home in McLean, a kind of housewarming he threw for himself.

This house had received considerable attention—there were various press reports that he was building something like the White House or Versailles, or the Great Gatsby mansion in the 1974 Robert Redford/Mia Farrow movie. While the property is large, Saylor claims the house is no big deal. "I live in a brick colonial house in McLean that was built on spec fifteen years ago. There is nothing special about it," he says.

The invitation was sent out by email to every employee of MicroStrategy on the Thursday evening before the party. It explained the Puff Daddy influence and made clear that it was a "Saylor-sponsored event," not a company one. He wrote in the email that sodas would be free, an inside joke referring to the fact that the company's new chief operating officer, brought in to tighten the financial reins, had recently thrown out Micro-Strategy's perk of giving unlimited free sodas to employees. "I have decided that it is time for another party, so I have decided to throw the All-Black Party at my new home in McLean. I have not yet moved into this place, so I figured it was a perfect venue to invite a few of my closest friends over for a good time. All MicroStrategists and their friends are invited," wrote Saylor.

About 1,500 people showed up, looking like either the hippest crowd in McLean or the largest funeral, depending on how you saw it. They arrived at the corner of Old Dominion and Spring Hill Road; from there shuttle buses took them to

Saylor's house. Huge tents were set up in the front and back of the property, and rugs, leather couches, and tables were rented for the occasion. Roses hung from the rafters, three truckloads of food were catered in, and thirty servers, a professional deejay, and five bartenders were on the scene. A photo station was set up to take people's pictures—about 400 or so. There was lots of dancing, drinking, and Saylor's favorite: "vigorous discussion."

Some of that was surely about the company's stock price, which wasn't doing much better.

On April 6, 2001, Saylor made the unusual move of pre-empting what he thought would be a string of negative stories about the company in *The Washington Post*. He sent a lengthy email to all MicroStrategy employees outlining what he thought these stories would be about and rebutting them. He believed one story would be about a spate of domain name acquisitions costing $3.2 million over a year for MicroStrategy. They regis-tered alarm.com, angel.com, speaker.com, michael.com, and many others. "Maybe we sell the domain Michael.com to Michael Jordan for marketing purposes . . . or Michael Jackson, if he ever does a comeback album ;-)" wrote Saylor. Saylor ended the letter by asking his employees to think "happy thoughts" and thanking them for their support.

One of the Capital Investors told Saylor that his experience is a Greek tragedy. "At that point the epiphany came to me that everyone's life is a Greek tragedy," said Saylor. "It's stupid to feel sorry for yourself. And it's arrogant and presumptuous to do so.

There is nobody in our world who is not going to go through a tragedy, even if they have an employee base of themselves . . . any business person who's been around for more than a few years has had setbacks, some of which are their own fault, some of which have nothing to do with them. They were on the wrong side of the street and got hit by a bus."

Eventually MicroStrategy raised $125 million in a private placement and $50 million from a Strategy.com placement. But even his closest friends and advisers still wince at his public statements such as the "shooting dogs" comments at the annual shareholders' meeting in July of 2001. His friends are trying. "He's demanding, he tends to rub people the wrong way," says Ramsey. He sighs. "He got carried away."

"Oh, he's the classic tragic figure," says Sachs. "But he never really had that money and he's still got millions. So we shouldn't feel *too* sorry for him."

Lately, people are wondering if Saylor will have to give up the CEO title. It's not clear what MicroStrategy's future holds—will it be bought by a larger company, survive on its own, or meet some other fate?

Either way, it would seem strange to separate Saylor and his company. "He is the company in many ways," says Sidgmore. "That's a strength and a weakness." As for finally listening to others with more experience—Sidgmore says it turns out that sometimes he does, sometimes he doesn't.

"He just leaves a lot of broken glass," says Ramsey.

In April of 2001, MicroStrategy said it was cutting a third of its 1,800-person staff. Strategy.com specifically was sliced from 180 to about 40. The same month, PricewaterhouseCoopers agreed to pay $55 million to settle the class-action lawsuit filed by the SEC alleging the accounting firm had defrauded investors by approving MicroStrategy's financial reports. But the firm denied any wrongdoing.

On September 14, three days after the terrorist attacks on the World Trade Center and the Pentagon, Saylor quietly pulled the plug on Strategy.com. All but a skeleton crew, who would physically shut down the network, were laid off. It was the end of the super-information system that was once Saylor's greatest ambition. In the midst of tragic images of people falling to their deaths and a nation poised on the brink of an uncertain war, the death of Strategy.com seemed inconsequential. It was a small sorrow, a MicroTragedy. That the end of the idea doesn't really matter is perhaps the worst pain in Saylor's shattered dream.

But Saylor's vaunted vision may not be gone yet. He is trying to do things a bit differently these days, with less emphasis on his personality and big-thinking and more on customers, revenues, and building technologies. When asked about one historical figure he has made reference to who was notoriously banished and then grandly returned, Saylor will not elaborate. "I have no thoughts about Napoleon," says Saylor. He does, however, have thoughts on how to describe his pain.

"What I've learned is that if you are a high-tech CEO, your

job is that of a cross between a celebrity and a politician and a business person, all combined into one," says Saylor. "You either have the best of all worlds or the worst of all worlds."

Saylor feels like he has to be elected again and again, every day, or the stock price goes through the floor. And he says he is trying to get used to reading rumors about himself that aren't true. He sighs.

"A celebrity can be strange and successful and their album will still sell. But when you're the CEO of a tech company, you can't hide," Saylor says sullenly.

Especially a public company. "If I was running a twenty-person operation I could say we're going to fly to the moon on blue Kool-Aid and people would think that's kind of cute and endearing. But when the stock hits 100, to say the same thing all of a sudden creates a liability, which was a simmering, festering one, which I think built up a lot of resentment and also created a liability which would come back and roost on us later on."

Andreessen says sometimes with creative, brilliant people like Saylor it's difficult to understand whether they are crazy or genius. "Sometimes you have to wait ten to twenty years to see which it is."

Saylor says he is spending more time these days diversifying, both psychologically and economically. He used to come into the office every Saturday and wonder why everyone else wasn't there, too. It isn't completely natural for him, but he is trying to become slightly less robotic, not as symbolic, and merely human. "He is still in tremendous pain," says Singh. "In some ways he was more naïve and in some ways more pure." For someone who aspires to greatness, however, "good" is never good enough. Whether that can satisfy Michael Saylor has yet to be seen. "The greater challenge," says Saylor, "is to manage the business in a technically humble fashion and still keep your ideals."

CHAPTER NINE

THE GREENFIELDS' HOUSE, POTOMAC, MARYLAND

May 2001

T HE POOL AND HOT TUB, surrounded by gray rocks and a small natural-looking waterfall, have just been installed for the summer at the Potomac home of Gary and Donna Greenfield. But it is the electronic "robot" that cleans the bottom of the pool, its long black arm meticulously canvassing the depths of the water, that is more fascinating to the Capital Investors. They are out on the Greenfield's terrace overlooking the pool on an early summer night, gathered for one of the group's occasional social events, at which married members arrive with their wives and the three bachelors of the group—Andreessen, Saylor, and Kimsey—can bring dates. The technology part of the pool-cleaner is interesting, the home improvement part as well. These are technologists with new money, and useful toys are of great interest. They lean over the patio railing with childlike curiosity and envy. *We need one of those.*

While much of Washington's high-tech rich has chosen Virginia, especially Great Falls and McLean, as home, the Greenfields reside across the Potomac River in an older rich–part of Washington, Potomac. This Maryland town is often described as horse country, which still feels right. But you're less likely to see livestock these days than another new all-mansion development.

After tuxedo-clad valets park the Capital Investors' cars down the street, the guests sip chardonnay and nibble mini-crabcakes, lobster rolls, satay chicken, and Peking duck in egg roll wrappers on the patio surrounded by huge trees. The wives are, mostly, extraordinarily career-driven, too, in areas such as education, real estate, and investing. One is a playwright, another a telecom executive and opera singer, and another a former Clinton staffer who started her own Internet company. It is a beautiful night and the Greenfields' three dogs—a sheep dog, a chocolate Lab, and a pug—run around examining each guest.

Jack McDonnell is excited about buying his company back and his wife, Jackie, jokes about dreading "going through this again." "This" means another initial public offering, that is, if things go well and if the market ever returns. The McDonnells had been semi-retired, living in Florida, before Jack's recent comeback. Al Berkeley's wife talks about a controversial new way of teaching reading to students. And they all discuss their children.

Sidgmore and Saylor powwow in a corner. It's been a tough week for Strategy.com, which has just announced it will lay off two-thirds of its staff. The employee base of that division of MicroStrategy, which numbered 180 in April, will be whittled down to about 40 by the end of the month.

Raj Singh and his wife, Neera, who is dressed in a colorful sari, mention in separate conversations that their current priority is "wealth preservation." Neera Singh says they're not making any new investments in the stock market these days, but trying to keep as much as they can of the telecom fortune she and her husband built. She asks Andrew Sachs and his wife, Heather, what their current investment strategy entails. This is one of those moments—like when everyone compares their private airplanes—when Sachs laughs and remembers he's not exactly like the men whose money he manages. He says right now they're focused on paying off Heather's law school loan, which was about $100,000 when she graduated. Neera Singh says she's surprised at how high educational debt can go.

Everyone moves inside for dinner. Three round tables are set up in the Greenfields' cavernous foyer. Staircases on either side lead to the second floor. The Greenfields are fond of modern art, especially acrylic and bronze sculptures by Frederick Hart. Vivid murals of gardens and flowerpots are painted on walls and in bathrooms. The tables are decorated with white lace tablecloths and gold and white china.

Somehow, as everyone sits down on the gold bamboo chairs, Andrew and Heather Sachs and Atlantic McClellan (the event-planner of the group) end up alone at one table. It's immediately apparent and people start to make jokes about the "kids' table." Marks is uncomfortable and asks the waiter to move the three into the other two tables. But Sachs and McClellan say never mind, they'll stay put, and laugh it off.

Art Marks and his wife, Nancy Casey, play off each other. Casey, a glamorous woman with short blonde hair who is wearing a sparkly dinner suit, runs a hedge fund that she recently moved from New York. She's been commuting for years and is thrilled to be back in their Potomac house and see more of her husband and their young children, three and six. Casey and Marks grill McDonnell about his deal, analyzing the numbers in detail and finally proclaiming it a good one. Casey says she tells bedtime stories to her kids featuring a character named Alan Greenspan, where he is alternately the bad guy or the good guy. Marks makes up stories, too, for his kids, spinning plots as he goes along.

Donna Greenfield is late to the shrimp and crab appetizer, her duty as a real-estate agent calling. She rushes back to the table, explaining that as much as the economy is faltering, real estate remains hot.

Saylor has been in his new mansion for one month and

talks about how strange it is to have enormous amounts of out-side space. He'd lived in a town house before. Saylor says he feels like the deer, the trees, and the shrubs are somehow all getting closer to his house and he's not quite sure how to control it all.

Conversations range from software to Prada clothing, from children's schools and college choices to the fall of PSINet.

A discussion about online grocery delivery services—Casey and Greenfield rely on Giant Food's Peapod—segues into how to spot a good business model. No one's quite sure anymore. They love the convenience of online grocery stores and are will-ing to pay for it. So why are some of the stores going out of busi-ness? Casey says she's happy Fernandez sold Proxicom when he did, that he'd increasingly have had trouble getting out.

The dogs are wandering the group, begging at each table. Donna Greenfield is upset, saying her daughter Brittany, a high-school student at Holton-Arms, was in charge of keeping the canines away tonight. Brittany, barefoot and in a sundress, hav-ing spent the day at a flower show with her boyfriend, finally pads in and pulls them away.

McDonnell, always the least politically correct, jokes about why Mandl skipped the dinner. "He could use a good meal," he says.

At the end of the evening, after the dessert and liquors, the guests mill leisurely around the front steps to wait for their cars. Saylor steps into his limousine, Berkeley and his wife climb into theirs for the trip back to their Baltimore home. Others have

BMWs, Mercedes. Marks has just bought a new convertible, a bright blue Lexus with a wood steering wheel. He's enormously proud of it and encourages Greenfield to take it for a spin. Greenfield says sure, jumps in, and peels out of his own drive-way into the summer night.

CHAPTER TEN

EXIT STRATEGIES

D EEP IN THE COLOMBIAN jungles, the leader of the largest Marxist guerrilla group in the region is wearing an AOL baseball cap with his traditional battle fatigues. He seems pleased with the gift from his visitor, AOL co-founder James Kimsey, whom Marulanda calls the "father of the American Internet."

Kimsey, a Clint Eastwood–type who looks tough, talks tough, and talks about being tough, is probably the closest Marulanda will ever come to the American Internet. In fact Kimsey and his friend, real-estate investor Joseph Robert, are the only Americans ever to visit Marulanda in his thirty years in the jungle. Not a huge surprise, considering the guerrillas are in a civil war that has left 30,000 people dead since the 1960s.

The multimillionaires traveled into the Colombian mountains to regale Marulanda with tales of capitalism and advise him, simply, to stop fighting and cease growing drugs. They ignored warnings from friends and government of the everyday dangers of kidnapping and murder in the country. Marulanda is the leader of the 16,000-strong rebel group known by the

Spanish acronym FARC, which occupies a Switzerland-size piece of land in the Colombian countryside.

"It's the kind of thing that's irresistible to me," Kimsey, an Army Ranger who served two tours in the Vietnam war, says later. "To talk to the oldest guerrilla in the world and try to persuade him of the wisdom of how the world is going to change."

One of the first questions an investor asks an entrepreneur is, "What's your exit strategy?" It means how they'll get out, and how they'll make money, usually a public offering or merger. Even as they were still experiencing the headiness of the Internet rush, members of the Capital Investors began casting about for their own way out, the big plan that would keep their legacy going. Few wanted to retire and most began to look for something even bigger as they managed their post-boom perceptions. In many cases what project or passion they choose shows more about them than the businesses that enabled them to embark on the new plan. "It's interesting to see who they want to become," says Sydney "Nini" Ferguson, a Washington lobbyist who has known many of the members for years.

"For me, parts of it were unsettling," says Robert about the trip into the Colombian jungles. "But for Rambo here," he nods at Kimsey, the danger "made it more interesting."

Since Kimsey, now in his early sixties, gave up his day job at AOL, he has been on a private diplomacy mission, meeting with Cuban leader Fidel Castro, accompanying President Clinton to

Vietnam, and visiting the president of Indonesia. No longer the chairman of a corporation, he's now chairman of Refugees International. Having been passed over for the post of ambassador to Vietnam, Kimsey has begun his own diplomatic campaigns, becoming a self-styled missionary of capitalism. But Colombia has a special interest for him.

First, it's difficult. That's a vital attribute. Colombia also affects the U.S. economy and culture through its drug trade. The American government has been helping Colombia more in recent years, most substantively with a $1.3-billion aid package. And, perhaps most importantly, Colombia has asked for Kimsey's help. "I'm a roving ambassador without portfolio and without control," says Kimsey. "I'm a soldier. I've always been a soldier."

Like many of the Capital Investors, Kimsey is in his post-wealth stage, where he's using his money and power to do something new. Some of the motivation comes from the guilt of huge success, some from a personality that is always searching. "You go through a lot of tough spots in your life and one day you wake up and realize, 'I didn't get killed. I'm exactly where I want to be.' And then there's this big voice going, 'Well?'"

Kimsey and Robert claim they aren't freelancing for the Central Intelligence Agency or anyone else, for that matter. Still, the FARC is on the U.S. list of international terrorists, and visiting them is not exactly recommended by the government. The State Department has tried to discourage their missions. "We can do things government officials can't do," says Kimsey. "We don't report to anybody."

Colombian President Andres Pastrana, a charming, intense man with a rapidly dwindling tenure and a huge problem to solve, doesn't know Steve Case. But through Colombia's ambassador in Washington, Luis Moreno, he met Kimsey, Robert, and Stephen Wolf, the chairman of US Airways.

On another trip to Colombia, Kimsey, Robert, Wolf, and Moreno travel on Robert's private plane, a Falcon 90, where lobster and champagne are served, using the finest china and Waterford crystal.

It's February and freezing in Washington, but as the plane lands at 2 A.M. in the seaside town of Cartagena, Colombia, the ocean breeze and twenty-four-hour salsa bands make it seem like it's summer all the time.

Bullet-proof Land Rovers escorted by government motorcades and secret service men dressed in short sleeves, but with telltale wires to their ears, pick up the businessmen and take them to Colombia's version of Camp David.

La Casa de Huespedes Illustres, "The House of Illustrious Guests," is a spectacular vacation mansion on the water. The grounds are full of fountains and secret pathways as well as red parrots and swaying palms.

The next day, meetings begin in an old stone fortress next to the mansion, poised on a hill overlooking the sea. Inside, the president and a group of fifteen business people from around the world, including Gustavo Cisneros, CEO of the Cisneros Group, and Minoru Makihara, CEO of Mitsubishi, will plan how to save Colombia.

Hanging over this meeting is a heightened tension about the peace process of the country. Pastrana has requested a meeting with Marulanda—it would be their third—and the group is expecting a yes or no to be delivered at any moment.

Pastrana, wearing a light pink oxford shirt, begins talking to the group, sitting at a long table in the fortress. He explains how the government has begun eradicating the coca and poppy fields and must find ways to replace illegal crop production in the economy. "This is a global problem that demands a global solution," says Pastrana.

One by one the top government officials of Colombia—trade, finance, and so on—give presentations to the group. It's like an investing road show. They are at once putting on their best performance while making it clear they desperately need money.

The minister of defense explains that they will add 10,000 soldiers this year, which will increase the army to 55,000. "We won't have as many high school soldiers," he says. "It is a waste of time because they can't be used to fight."

On huge overhead displays, the country's public opinion polls show what groups as disparate as the Catholic church, the media, and the two rebel forces think about Pastrana. The one thing these groups have in common: Pastrana is not that popular across the board.

There are more slides on helicopter fleet increases and the cost to the country for cocaine seizures.

"I know fellows like Jim Kimsey are familiar with this kind of money, but for us it is a lot of money," says one of the officials.

They talk about the deep problems in the country related to the drug trade: kidnapping, extortion, money laundering.

Pastrana jumps in, saying that FARC has recently recruited many young men, and the total force is now estimated at 16,000. His hand shakes as he says that number. "It is very difficult to control this type of terrorism," he says.

The minister of finance shows Colombia's credit ratings, back up from a time when the country was the equivalent of Russian junk bonds. "Mr. Robert, I can almost guarantee if you invest in real estate here you'll make a killing," he says.

But that's a tough sell. "What proactive steps are you taking to encourage this investment?" asks Kimsey. "People don't get up in the morning and say, 'Boy, I'm going to invest in Colombia today.'"

"We have to change the perception," admits the minister.

Then, as the discussion turns to information technology, a note is handed to Pastrana, a memo that has come by fax. He reads it, puts it down, reads it again, shows it to the person next to him. He nods yes to his wife, a beautiful blonde woman in a multicolored top and yellow pants who is sitting across from him at the table. This is her way of life. Her father was kidnapped and killed when she was younger, and her husband was taken by a drug cartel when he was mayor of Bogota, but escaped. Pastrana joked afterward that after traveling over so many potholes in the trunk of a car he knew he had to pay better attention to fixing the roads.

Some saw the note arrive, but most of the table is still talking about the Internet. Cisneros advises giving every Colombian a computer and having the government pay for Internet access.

Pastrana lets the discussion come to an end and then says he'd like to read from a letter he's just received from Marulanda. The note is in Spanish, but he reads a few parts in English.

"I express my interest to hold a new meeting . . . so that we deal with the exchange of prisoners . . . I suggest we meet next February 8 because . . . the security makes it impossible to hold the meeting when you suggest."

It is a delay, and no one is sure what will come of it, but still, the answer is yes. The peace process will move at least this much forward. Everyone claps and there is much excitement and nervousness in the room.

Kimsey and Robert, ever the adventurers, say they want to go, too. But one of Pastrana's aides says not this time; the president will likely travel to the camp with only one bodyguard and an assistant.

The doors to the fortress open wide into the bright sun and the group spills out into the grass. The Colombian newspaper and television crews, clearly alerted to the news, rush to the president.

Most of the group walk to a courtyard under palm trees

with bright blooming flowers, where large round tables have been set for lunch. Shrimp and other seafood are served with a sweet coconut rice with raisins, banana rolls, beef, salad, and coffee.

Afternoon presentations are more relaxed, although there is an air of great expectation. A representative of McDonald's in Colombia speaks, saying about the country, "With all that manure, there's got to be a pony in here somewhere."

Kimsey smiles to himself. AOL-watchers know he has always said the same thing (with a different word for *manure*) about America Online throughout its troubles.

A theme of the afternoon is the perception of Colombia in the United States and the rest of the world.

"Colombia has a terrible image," says Kimsey. "The first time I came here someone said if I didn't come back could they have my stuff."

"Now that CNN is AOL we hope the tide will be with us," responds Pastrana, an overt plea for these Americans, at least, to say good things about Colombia.

That night, some of the group, followed diligently by multiple bodyguards, celebrate the planned meeting between Marulanda and Pastrana at a bar in Cartagena. Hips are swiveling to the hot salsa music and tangerine juice and vodka cocktails are flowing.

"It's the make or break of the peace process," says Moreno, a short, funny man who is dancing with anyone who will be his partner, including his wife, a former trade minister to Venezuela. Many of the bar patrons recognize Moreno, and they have heard today's news. "Viva Colombia!" says one woman who dances up to Moreno and clinks glasses with him.

On the way out, Kimsey leaves the waitress a $100 bill for a $10 tab. "Over-tipping cures communism," he says, smiling, as if he is repeating a proverb.

These trips began as Kimsey moved farther away from AOL. After grooming Steve Case to run the company, Kimsey turned over the CEO reigns to him in 1992 and resigned from the board in 1997. When AOL bought Time Warner, he also stepped off the board of the AOL Time Warner Foundation. Kimsey runs his own $70-million private foundation, chairs the Washington Opera, and is a trustee of the Kennedy Center. And he's part of an investment group trying to bring a baseball team to Washington. But with no particular day-to-day company responsibilities and millions to spend, Kimsey began traveling. He regularly goes back to Vietnam where he still funds an orphanage. He says it wasn't really his intent to finance the institution, but a group of nuns aggressively pursued him until he gave in.

Holidae Hayes, his ex-girlfriend of eight years, says Kimsey, like many of the Capital Investors, is on a quest. But his war experience makes him crave a different level of physical danger. "After Vietnam, nothing will replicate that experience," says Hayes. "He goes through life kicking over buckets looking for adventure."

Since he and Hayes broke up, Kimsey has become one of Washington's most eligible bachelors, appearing regularly in the social pages of newspapers where he is often promoting favorite charities. At these events, one of his favorite companions is Queen Noor.

But Kimsey doesn't charm everyone on his my-way-or-the-highway path. The U.S. State Department tried to talk Kimsey out of going to the Colombian jungles.

"We discouraged him, pointing out this is a dangerous place," says a State Department official who met with Kimsey before the trip. "Since the FARC is responsible for a number of acts of terrorism against Americans, we feel it is risky business." Since their trips, the peace process has been stalled and started and stalled again, and continuous reports of violence serve as persistent reminders that in many places, especially Colombia, change is difficult to make happen.

And the relationship between Kimsey and Case has chilled since Kimsey, long one of the more open AOL executives with the press, began to undermine the credit that Case was single-handedly receiving for saving AOL. Kimsey told many reporters he would fear leaving AOL in Case's care if it weren't for Bob Pittman coming in to save the day. "I could have never left without Bob," Kimsey said.

Kimsey also takes pride in pointing out that AOL is in the Washington area because that's where he grew up, and that's where he wanted AOL to live, too. "If it was up to Steve Case, he would have moved it to Silicon Valley," Kimsey says.

Mostly, the two are cordial and they occasionally appear together at events. They are almost like brothers now: knowledge of each other and jealousy run deep. They have shared an experience that few others understand. "AOL is like one of my kids," says Kimsey. "You send it to college. You want it to be all it can be. You don't want to take it home."

But he's thinking about other things these days, mainly diplomacy and sports. "We won't tolerate failure. Everything is first class, first rate," says Kimsey. "Can I get a summit for the Colombian peace process? Can I get a baseball team to Washington? That gets my juices going."

All of the Capital Investors have before them a daunting challenge: How do they manage their image, their legacy—post-boom and post-crash. They want to avoid suggestions that they are arrogant. But Internet visionaries became business charlatans in the press and in the eyes of their investors overnight. The harshest criticism is coming from those who never believed, or cashed in on, the Internet frenzy. And it's also pouring in from overseas, where the heights were never so mountainous. Morino saw this at the annual World Economic Forum, where international leaders convene once a year to discuss all matters of importance. "There was a natural tension between the old- and new-economy players," recalled Morino. "One banker said, 'The Americans aren't so smart now, are they?' He was right. The people began to smoke their own fumes." And it is not so smooth on the way down, as some, such as Michael Saylor, have learned. "The minute you fall, they come after you," says Morino. "Ask Michael."

While he worries that pride will spoil much of what technologists were trying to accomplish, Morino is also pleased to see how some are using their money in other ways now. "The power of the money is being felt," says Morino. Befitting the end of an era, most of the Capital Investors made a major professional change in the late 1990s to early 2000s. Some, such as Michael Saylor, Bill Melton, and Alex Mandl, saw their companies crumble around them. Jeong Kim of Lucent worked relentlessly to keep up morale and stock prices before jumping to an "honorable profession" as an engineering professor at his alma mater, the University of Maryland. Kim had agreed to spend three years at Lucent after it bought his company, Yurie Systems, for $1 billion. At the end of his tenure, Lucent offered Kim the top job at Bell Labs. But Kim was holding out for CEO of Lucent, which was not offered. He opted to teach instead. It's "back to normal" but it's hard to go "back" to anything after this experience.

———————

"You want to do something significant," says Mandl, as he explored what to do after Teligent. "Something that has breakthrough possibilities." In the next company, he plans to control the board and he will most likely regularly sell off shares, even though analysts and investors don't always like to see executives do so. Mandl has been exploring what he calls some "expensive lessons." There is a half a billion dollars to consider. "I didn't sell one share," he says. "I felt it was the wrong thing to do. In hindsight, some would call it stupid. You certainly have a right to take some of it off the table."

Greenfield decided to leave Merant and in September the entire company announced it would move to Oregon. Fernandez sold Proxicom and he and Leonsis became sports impresarios. Case ascended to the chairmanship of the largest media empire in the world, but began to keep an even lower profile than before. The Capital Investors agree Case's timing was best of them all. "The guy who survives buys real assets, like Steve Case," says Mandl. Ramsey started his hedge fund ("We're all about buying dollar bills for 20 or 30 or 40 cents," he says cheerily) and McDonnell took over his old company.

Marks says he cycles between chasing the next thing and being happy. Immediately after leaving venture capital fund New Enterprise Associates, he did the happy stage, planting 80,000 bulbs at his Potomac house—"It looks like Monet's garden,"—and then spending a bit more than a month with his family in France. It took most everyone in the technology community by surprise to hear Marks was leaving NEA. Although neither side will go into details, it seems to have been a clash of personalities and business styles. Marks says the founding partners of NEA walked into his office one day in the summer of 2001 and said: "We decided we don't like you and we've decided you should leave."

"There was a fit issue," says Peter Barris, managing general partner for NEA's Reston office. Marks was asked to retire but he wasn't ready. He was completely taken by surprise and spent several days writing a letter to try to patch things up, to no avail. "It's just like a divorce from a spouse who hasn't told you she has a lover on the side," says Marks.

But he's already got a new thing: a venture capital fund, Valhalla Partners, named after the lodge he and his wife stayed in in Alaska on their honeymoon. He's been shopping the idea to investors he'd want in the $150-million fund, and says so far he's received good reaction. And he's searching for partners to help him on the new quest. "Small is everything," says Marks about his new project, meaning number of partners, investors, and investments. "Everybody got overcommitted," he says of the crazy days of venture capital fund-raising and investment.

Although NEA is slowing a bit these days, it is still moving at a faster clip than in most previous years. Barris says NEA is investing at half the pace of the 1999/2000 time period, which was three times faster than the previous five years.

Steve Walker, also a venture capitalist, watched many of his investments through Walker Ventures disintegrate. "I thought we were going down a little river and it turned out to be Niagara Falls," he says.

While he still makes investments, Walker began to focus more attention on a fun project, Capitol Rising, a helicopter service. Walker is a former Pentagon engineer who became a multimillionaire in 1998 when he sold his security software company, Trusted Information Systems, for $350 million to Network Associates. Walker then started a venture capital fund designed to encourage and harvest the youngest ideas. With white hair and years of experience, Walker became a grandfatherly influence on many young Washington executives. He uses the word "cool" often and giggles, especially when he is talking about one of his helicopters. When Walker made his money, his estate attorney advised him to spend some that would change his lifestyle. Walker bought a red jet ski and was looking around for something else. He'd been complaining that it would take him and his wife two and a half hours driving on a good day to get to the Rehoboth beach house they'd bought in 1996 to celebrate the IPO of his company. He saw a helicopter near their Glenwood, Maryland, home one day and thought, this is it. He now has three, Skywalker I, II, and III, a play off his own name and the *Star Wars* character.

On a forty-five-minute ride from Tysons Corner to Tipton, Maryland, where he rents a hangar for his helicopters, Walker points out the CIA, Jefferson Memorial, and other highlights like a proud tour guide. He doesn't have an aviation background and certainly doesn't fly the helicopters himself, but employs a full-time pilot. Walker likes to sit in the front seat and watch the world go by through the clear globe surrounding him.

The business plan for this hobby involves creating an air taxi service for executives who either don't have private planes or just need to make a quick trip. Walker's customers include fellow Capital Investors Fernandez, Mandl, Kimsey, Melton, and Saylor, who on one trip took aerial pictures of his new property. Walker charges between $650 and $1,700 an hour, based on which of the three helicopters you choose. Capitol Rising's advertising brochure features a picture of Walker and one of his planes, asking "Where may we take you today?" an unmistakable play on Microsoft's advertising pitch. There is a major glitch, however, in his plans. To run a helicopter service, you need approved places to take off and land, known as "helistops." Turns out that homeowners and local politicians don't love Walker's idea as much as he does. Walker's plans to build helistops in Tysons Corner near the Ritz-Carlton and in Reston incurred the wrath of area residents who worry about the noise and don't like the idea of a taxi service for the rich flying over their homes.

"I started out doing this purely for fun," says Walker. "And then it became a challenge. How do I find these helistops? It's the hardest thing I've ever done."

———————————

Raul Fernandez is tan. He still has a paunch but he has lost weight after working out with a trainer during the summer of 2001, preparing for a triathlon, trying to get down to his "pre-IPO weight."

The television in his Reston office is tuned to the Wimbledon finals, not the all-financial news channel CNBC. "I don't watch the ticker anymore," he says. On Wall Street, PXCM no longer exists.

Up until a couple of days before, he still cared. Fernandez said he'd stay with the company for three years, integrating the teams and carrying the flag. But in June, Dimension Data missed its quarterly numbers for the first time ever. No one told Fernandez to expect that blow—he read it on Yahoo that morning like everyone else. Being entirely out of the loop was hard to take for a guy used to running the show. "I haven't worked for anyone in ten years," he says. But what was worse was that as a condition of the deal, he was required to buy a certain amount of stock over a ten-day period, which he did right before the earnings announcement. Fernandez bought $7 million of Dimension Data and its value fell almost immediately to $4 million. Had he known about the missed earnings, he could have bought at another time. His new bosses knew he was buying then and didn't stop him. He sees it as a $3-million slap in the face. "I'm pretty mad," he says, simmering with anger. "They violated the trust. They knew I had a gun to my head. My tenure here will be shorter than I thought."

Fernandez is talking about taking a six-month trip around the world with his wife, who has put up with her husband going on scores of overseas business trips during the first year of their marriage. He'll advise Dimension Data officially for a while after he quits coming to the office every day. Fernandez will join General Atlantic, a venture capital firm that funded Proxicom early on and where Mario Morino is a special partner. General Atlantic's Washington offices are in the familiar cocoon of the Morino building.

Fernandez says he's done being a player and wants to coach. He's got a hockey team to work with, and the chance—which would become reality—that his partner Michael Jordan may play basketball again is fueling excitement. And in fact, the week following the DiData surprise, Fernandez and his partner, Ted Leonsis, landed the biggest deal so far of their careers as hockey owners. They spent $30 million to get one of the top scorers in the game, Jaromir Jagr. The deal was sweeter because they took Jagr from the arch-rival Pittsburgh Penguins. In Washington, where hockey has never been a top-line sport, the news was big. Front page news stories heralded the deal as the biggest thing in the Caps' twenty-seven-year history. "I view this as another step in building the city," said Leonsis at a press conference that day on the basketball practice court at the MCI Center. With Fernandez at his side, Leonsis joked about how he was able to pull $30 million seemingly out of his back pocket. "I lost more money yesterday with AOL stock than in buying Jagr. I won't buy a boat. I was thinking of buying a yacht and instead I got Jagr." They would later announce the deal had been extended to keep Jagr for five years at $11 million annually.

Fernandez is slightly bitter about the way things ended with Proxicom, but he knows he has to be happy overall. He figures he made about $220 million on this Internet ride, with everything he has cashed out since 1996. And he has seen many others fall by the wayside. At one point, he was worth $1.1 billion. "It's wild to look around and see where everything is," he says quietly. "It happened so fast."

As many journeys as Morino has begun, he says his current one is what all the others have been leading up to. "He's been looking for the right vessel for his ideas," says former employee Liz Wainger.

It's an attempt to change philanthropy. For this project, Morino has asked his friends in Capital Investors for money. First, Morino put up $10 million himself. Fernandez and Warner agreed to co-found Venture Philanthropy Partners, Fernandez putting up $4 million and Warner an undisclosed amount. Sidgmore, Kimsey, and Kim, too, were early supporters.

"In software, he's made more money than anyone needs," says Esther Smith about what motivates Morino now. "But in philanthropy, he could go beyond that. He wants to be a global leader."

Still, Morino hates what he calls the "ask," petitioning his friends for money. He says he never personally did fund-raising for the Potomac KnowledgeWay because he thought he'd have one chance. "Netpreneur was to build a bridge to entrepreneurs," he says. "We knew there would be an ask later on." Although he probably didn't know the ask would happen just as the economy was faltering. Regardless, by the end of 2001, Morino had collected $25 million for the first fund earmarked for children's causes, plus $10 million more committed, not including the financing he put up himself.

An example of how the connection came full circle is web-Methods. Morino never invested in the company, but helped them through advice and introductions. Before he could approach company founders and husband and wife team Phillip Merrick and Caren DeWitt, they called him to get involved and to learn how to set up their own foundation.

He calls what he has created "structured chaos." But while many are embracing Morino's new brand of philanthropy, he is aware that those who have been running charities for years will be skeptical of his ideas. But he believes they need to do things differently.

"The whole nonprofit mechanism today is very frail," Morino says. "People are running on fumes and hearts instead of infrastructure."

Morino's first fund will invest in Washington-based causes and organizations, because he believes giving is tied to geography. He says the fund's philosophy and encouragement of learning from each other is similar to what Capital Investors does. He will have dinners for the funders of VPP, too. VPP members will take board seats related to their "investments"—

don't call them donations. And they'll treat them like a business, with attention to regular reports and the bottom line. For Morino, this is about more than helping a few children's organizations.

"We're trying to affect philanthropy itself," says Morino. "Why do all this if there's not a quantum change? I don't understand saving a single starfish."

Morino knows traditional philanthropists might feel insulted by his ideas, which basically call for an overhaul of the system.

"Don't come across the line saying you have the answers to all the world's problems," he tells himself. "Then you have a hand grenade in your hands."

But he says most of his friends don't connect with donating to a museum or theater group. They want impact, return on investment. And they want it in their lifetime. "You know these minds," says Morino. "They say, 'Give me something big to solve.' They're attracted to that."

They are also increasingly worried about what they'll leave behind.

"I fear that I'll die early and it will all go to the Morino Institute or Uncle Sam. I've had that discussion with twenty individuals," Morino says.

Warner is a founding board member, along with Raul Fernandez, of VPP. "It struck me how many of these nonprofits had almost a complete lack of infrastructure. No management team, no procedures in place," says Warner. "They may have a great idea and a passionate leader, but their ability to grow to scale or leverage any of their assets was basically nonexistent."

What's unusual here is that foundations used to be the realm only of the older rich and of just a few families. The high-tech wealth has changed that. "The phenomenal thing, the historical thing, is that people in their thirties are making philanthropy part of their lives," says Gary Jonas of VPP.

"The idea of simply writing a check doesn't get people excited anymore," agrees Warner.

Art Marks says he trusts Morino because of what he's done for the community. Of course he invested. But Marks thinks Morino waited too long to raise the money, took too long to study every detail, and hit the fund-raising stride just as technology companies were decimated. Some may pull back their investments and others who have committed stock watched much of what they've given lost in value. The shares of stock Marks put aside for VPP are now worth much less, he says.

One year after Saylor's speech about the online university, Fernandez is the speaker at the same *Washington Business Journal* philanthropy summit. Saylor does not attend, and it does not seem any work has been done on his university. Saylor is reluctant to talk about it, and it's not at all clear if the project will again emerge.

Fernandez talks about his $4-million investment in Venture Philanthropy Partners. He says when Proxicom went public in

1999, he looked for a philanthropy for dummies book, but couldn't find one. His father, who emigrated from Cuba in the 1950s when Castro took power, gave Fernandez a book on the Carnegie tradition of philanthropy. "We help management refine missions and develop goals," he says of how he'll work with a nonprofit on behalf of VPP, not exactly the traditional way of donating to charity.

There were other changes. Just as the market was falling apart, Morino did something unusual, something that he tried to keep fairly quiet. The godfather of Washington, the guy who promoted the area to the rest of the world, moved out of town. He still shows up at events, meetings, and around Reston and Tysons Corner. He'll often fly in on his private plane for an evening or afternoon, so no one would notice he's going home to Cleveland rather than Great Falls. But his real home is back in Ohio; his kids go to school and play soccer there. He did this in part because he felt Cleveland was a more "real" place to raise his kids.

"There's a sense of pretentiousness that pervades the region," says Morino.

Others agreed. "Living in Northern Virginia is a sanitizing experience," says Esther Smith. "You never meet anyone poor. It's like being on an army post."

But if Morino and Case were going lower-profile in Washington, AOL Time Warner executive Leonsis was showing up more and more, almost incessantly.

Leonsis, a big, friendly bear of a guy, likes to get things done and cross them off his list. This is not a "take out the garbage" kind of list, but a "meet Mickey Mantle" kind of list. Leonsis began "The List," as he and his friends call it, in his twenties after a terrifying airplane trip, when he thought he wouldn't make it back alive. There are 101 things he wants to do before he dies. Some goals are entirely reasonable, the things many people would put on such a list. Visit Paris. Play Pebble Beach. See the Rolling Stones. Get married.

Others show his particular interests. Restore an antique auto. Have a building or perpetual memorial named after the Leonsis family. Be worth a billion dollars, after taxes. Start a company and sell it. So far, 66 of the 101 items have little check marks next to them, although Leonsis has added and subtracted items as he's grown older.

Twenty-six of the goals are sports-related. Leonsis has caught a foul ball and gone to a US Open tennis final. He has not won a world championship or hit a hole in one. Yet. Snagging Jaromir Jagr to play for the Capitals could, possibly, help on the Stanley Cup quest.

And then in September of 2001, Leonsis and Fernandez announced that after many rumors and much debate, Michael Jordan would return to play for their basketball team, the Washington Wizards. Jordan has agreed to be paid $1 million a year for a five-year deal, which he will donate to charity. "It'll be an exciting time," says Fernandez. "The ingredients for a great sports town are here."

Jordan's return was treated like the second coming. But it wasn't at all clear that he'd be in top form, especially after an accident right before his announcement. "The rib injury did set him back . . . but there's no way he'll make a fool of himself," says Fernandez. Although it was one of the worst-kept secrets the weeks before the announcement that Jordan was coming back, he delayed his press conference, originally scheduled for the Monday after the September 11 attacks.

Getting Jordan was all about making the right business deal. Jordan had to agree to divest his stake because there are league rules that players cannot be owners. Jordan chose to sell his shares back to Leonsis. "We come from a culture of giving up equity to create value," says Fernandez, who still remembers how difficult it was the day he was no longer majority owner of Proxicom. "That's why he came."

But the owners claim Jordan has no promises that he'll get his share back when he re-retires. "Of course we will talk to him," says Leonsis. "But there are no guarantees. It's against the rules."

Anybody wondering what Leonsis might be up to in the coming years should take another look at the unchecked items on The List. Own a mountain home. Make a movie. Live overseas. Take a year sabbatical. Go into outer space.

September 11 was AOL's single best sign-up day in its history. When people, especially in New York and Washington, couldn't get through by phone, they checked in successfully on email. "Are you there? Are you okay?" These important questions flew around via emails and instant messages. Leonsis was at AOL in Dulles, Virginia, that day. He tried to call the Capitals office, but couldn't get through. He reached them on a Black-Berry and told the players and managers to go home. "We're ingrained now. We're a public trust and utility," says Leonsis.

Still, two weeks after the tragedy, AOL Time Warner warned it would not meet its financial targets for not only that year, but the following year as well. Advertising revenues were falling and suddenly the media Goliath seemed vulnerable on many fronts. Merrill Lynch downgraded the company from "buy" to "neutral." The merger, so far, could not be called a success.

After September 11, Fernandez began looking for gas masks on eBay. McDonnell decided to fly more on his time-share personal jet than on commercial flights. Dave Holtzman had nightmares. And Marks started seeing the "terrorist tax" pop up all around in slowed business deals, delayed investments, and the paralysis of risk taking.

"Some of the excesses of the late 1990s seem even more exaggerated now," says Fernandez. "There is a whole reassessment of everything. Do you plan for another attack in this quarter?" Fernandez, whose wife was pregnant with their first child when the attacks occurred, decided not to purchase gas masks after all, because he decided that was buying into the fear.

The Capital Investors invited a terrorism expert to speak at their October meeting. Most in the group said they left the dinner more shaken than when they walked in. Silver says that evening he came home and told his wife everything the expert had said. Neither of them slept that entire night. Many of the Capital Investors had completely stopped flying commercial— "I know everybody on the airplane,"—says McDonnell when he uses his own.

Hayes sent a note to her clients saying that throughout history, times of crisis have opened economic opportunity.

That's just what Ramsey was thinking on September 17, the first day the markets were open after the attacks. That day, he bought stock in rapidly falling travel companies Travelocity and Sabre—"a couple million" in each. Several weeks later when anthrax started showing up in post offices, Ramsey increased a stake he already had in an email marketing company called Digital Impact. He figured direct marketing, along with everything else that depended on snail mail, would take a hit. "Certainly email is less hazardous to your health," he says.

Sidgmore, who thought Ramsey's idea to focus on distressed companies was a smart idea even before the attacks, signed on to New Enterprise Associates to become a venture capitalist, in what many saw as a counterintuitive time to become a professional investor. "There will be huge opportunities over the next few years," says Sidgmore. "The economy is not going to turn around anytime soon. We've been preparing for economic war."

But it was not always easy to capitalize on damaged companies. In November of 2001, a potential buyout of Teligent, which had been operating under Chapter 11, by a group backed by the company's existing management, fell through. Teligent shut down its sales operations and sent its remaining customers letters informing them they would be transferred to other phone carriers. The company that once had 3,600 employees now had just a skeleton crew still trying to sell what was left of the business. They hadn't yet filed for liquidation, but the situation looked grim.

No one was sure of anything. "I used to be able to smell a deal," says Greenfield. "Now you can't tell."

After the Internet crash, and even more as the United States became engaged in a war, the old-style of Washington technology came back. "Fortune One" was always the biggest technology customer, after all. In November of 2001, Andreessen was going through a top-secret security clearance for a contract with an "unnamed three-letter" agency of the government. "The war on terrorism needs information processing," says Andreessen. He says it's funny he's actually excited that Loudcloud has jumped to trading around $3 a share.

For the moment, expectations were lower and style was lower-key. Mario and Dana's holiday party in December of 2001 had no theme, no costumes. The invitation "to come together at this important time with family and friends" was a simple cream-colored card with small gold snowflakes, compared with last years' four-page roaring '20's newsletter invitation with joke stories about the "Morino Gang," and a number called the "hooch hotline" to RSVP. That invitation read *Come! Or sleep with the fishes.*

Morino was beginning to worry that the economy and the war would tear philanthropists away from continuing social services work.

Still, as economists finally began saying the "recession" word and business was dreary, there was one party most of the Capital Investors had backed with their money, contacts, and if they lived in Virginia, their vote. And they were ready for a celebration.

CHAPTER ELEVEN

CITRONELLE,
WASHINGTON, D.C.

May 2001

A N EARLY SUMMER EVENING at one of Washington's best restaurants, Citronelle, sees the group in better spirits. The warm weather in Georgetown is without humidity; the rose-colored walls, yellow and teal leather chairs, and flower arrangements in Citronelle's "Christal" room are luxuriously cheering. And those who have had the roughest past month have not shown up.

Since the group last met, Alex Mandl stepped down from his chief executive role at Teligent and Michael Saylor's Strategy.com division slashed two-thirds of its staff. Saylor has also begun suing Internet chat-room frequenters for defaming him, moving *The Wall Street Journal* to run a caricature of Saylor with an enormous head and huge, bulging cheeks.

Raul Fernandez is also absent, although he did not have a bad month at all. After almost a year of watching his company's value plummet, he sold Proxicom to South African company Dimension Data. Fernandez made $90 million personally in the sale and is gearing up to focus more on being a sports mogul and private investor.

Tonight, there's a new member in the group, Nigel Morris, a Brit in a natty pin-striped suit who was a punk rocker in London during a former life. Morris says he came to the United States with a curiosity for the American way of doing business. There's room for Morris because Andreessen, who moved to Palo Alto after joining, and Spoon, who relocated to Boston, have decided not to continue investing in future funds. But they're still considered members, their money remains in the companies they've invested in so far, and they are invited to dinners.

As the cocktail hour begins, Warner stirs up the energy in the room, working it like a political event. He's shaking hands, slapping backs, making sure he speaks with each person. "Mark's asking for money again," says Ramsey as he watches Warner move.

Bill Gorog says he's had a particularly great day. He spent it in New York with Al Berkeley, where Gorog's son's company, Roxio, which makes CD-burning software, went public on the Nasdaq stock market. "They have real profits," says Gorog proudly. Melton says he's impressed Roxio could get out at all in this market, one of the worst for initial public offerings in recent history.

Melton's exhausted. A year and a half ago, when he resigned his CyberCash board seat, he intended to retire and spend most of his time in Paris, where he and his playwright wife have a home. Now, he sighs, "I got called back. I'm on the board of twelve companies and all of them have issues." He's examining each one now to figure out which should live and which should die. The demise of CyberCash has drained him, not only of some of his optimism but of millions he personally put into the company. "Twenty-five million and five years of my life, it's worth an aspirin or two," he says. Melton likens starting a company to gambling. "You pay your money, you play the game, and you find out."

The members are all seated at a long table with a white cloth, green and white china, and purple, orange, and yellow blossoms in low vases. "Before Andrew talks to us about our first overpriced deal . . ." begins Ramsey. Certainly, from the investors' point of view, most deals are bargains these days. And entrepreneurs are willing to sell chunks of their creations at much lower prices. Warner introduces Morris. He says in Morris, the group gets "brains, brawn, and beauty."

"It's a blessing that Nigel has come here with probably inappropriate expectations," says Ramsey. The group's faltering companies have become somewhat of an inside joke. "We eat nice meals," adds Sidgmore.

Morris gives a brief rundown on the consumer lending company he co-founded and is president of, Capital One, which is best known for its credit cards. He explains that Capital One went public in 1994 and has about 40 million household customers. "It's a pretty big old thing," he says in his British accent. "We're the most profitable unrecognizable brand." Several of the members know Morris and lobbied for his membership, most notably Kimsey, who is on the board of directors of Capital One.

McDonnell and others begin, almost absentmindedly, to heckle Morris. "Jack never behaves," says Ramsey. "This is a member, not a [presenting] company," reminds Berkeley. Morris goes on to explain a Capital One deal with Kmart. "And they're all married to their sisters," blurts McDonnell.

Warner stands up with a glass of wine and invites everyone in the group to join him later that evening at the opening of a new restaurant he has invested in, The Majestic Café, in Alexandria, Virginia, which Warner calls "God's country." Several members of the group make fun of Warner for his transformation into country-boy politician. Warner laughs and brags that he even sponsors a NASCAR race car now and went turkey-hunting on a recent day at 5 A.M. "You'll do anything," says Berkeley, shaking his head.

Then Warner makes the pitch: "I'll put it like this. You can invest in the restaurant or you can put more toward the campaign." He's serious, of course.

Warner says he has a tough 176 more days ahead. "This is the longest road show of my life. I want to thank you. It's the hardest thing I've ever done. Having the job will be easier than getting the job."

"Will you remember our names?" asks Al Berkeley. "Yes, Bill," responds Warner. The group claps and Warner makes his exit. His friends won't see as much of him over the next few months, unless they hang out at his fund-raisers and political debates.

Tonight the group hears from one new company looking for money and two firms already in the Capital Investors portfolio, here to give updates.

MaTRICS, a firm founded by former National Security Agency scientists, uses radio frequencies to develop a sophisticated tracking system for products shipped by businesses. MaTRICS' president, Laura Neuman, walks in with the rest of her team, who all stand by the wall. Neuman explains that the chips are the size of a grain of sand, that they have nine patents, that they have competitors but believe they are ahead so far of any rivals.

"Hey Laura, what's the range advantage?" asks Sidgmore.

Berkeley asks about her background. Silver asks what could go wrong.

Dinner arrives, either salmon in leek and truffle sauce or filet mignon with napoleon potatoes and truffles. Berkeley has ordered whatever is the lowest-fat meal they could round up.

"Laura, let me ask you the hard question," says Ramsey. "I know Digex well and they never hit a number. Why will you be different?"

"It's always about execution," she says. "The challenge is freezing a product in a space and time. It's always about the team."

Berkeley leans forward. "Talk dirty, technically," he orders.

She launches into an explanation of how the technology works. Her colleagues jump in but there's something missing. Finally she admits that they are intentionally being cautious because Art Marks's venture capital company, New Enterprise Associates, has an investment in one of MaTRICS' key competitors. "I'll be happy to leave the room if you'll explain it to someone else," says Marks.

"You've gone 100 miles ahead and the market has gone 100 miles backward," warns Melton. Some of the members are worried, too, that the company is worth, or valued, at a higher price than their regular investments.

"I think your presentation's great but your valuation's out of sight," says McDonnell.

Sachs says it's time to cut it off, everyone claps and the group leaves the room.

"That's one impressive woman," says Sidgmore.

"It's hard to make a decision when you've fallen in love," quips Berkeley.

And then the group launches into a heated discussion about just what kinds of deals they should be doing. They agree it's a good company, better than many they've seen. But it's a bit further ahead than some would like to see in an investment, and definitely more expensive.

"This is outside the limits of our structure," says McDonnell.

Sachs says he has been purposely bringing in later-stage companies because, especially during an economic downturn, he thinks the group won't give the go-ahead on the early ones that have so much yet to prove.

"That's a mistake," says Gorog. "If we don't find a deal in three months, that's okay. We need the three guys in their basement."

Ramsey interjects that Sachs culls through about 200 business plans a month and that the group should go over its mission more carefully soon, but not now. Marks and Berkeley say they like the deal.

"So they're screwed," says Berkeley. "Everyone and their uncle is screwed these days."

David Giannini of Core Communications walks in next. Sachs prefaces the presentation by saying the company is actually doing well. Everyone cheers. Giannini says he's here tonight to tell the group what he's doing with their money. He talks about deals he has done, including a new one with Opryland. The Capital Investors clap, good work, keep it up, smiles around the table.

Giannini leaves. "He's a fantastic sales guy," says Silver, whose venture firm has also invested in Core. "He just goes, goes, goes."

"What's the exit?" asks Marks.

"They won't IPO," says Silver. He says the company has been approached by a lot of companies about an acquisition, but the time's not right . . . yet.

Next up is David Holtzman, former chief technologist at domain name registrar Network Solutions. He has a start-up called Opion—a technical way to search for and analyze buzz on the Internet—that the group has already funded. Holtzman is casual, low-key. He admits that when Capital Investors gave him money, the business plan hadn't been completely formed. He's back tonight to update the group on the company and how their $300,000 has been put to work.

"Now," he says, "we've got a patent on determining a person's influence." Holtzman figures there are 30 million people who regularly converse on or read message boards. He says he can personally identify 3 million of them.

Opion started selling its software two weeks ago, but it hasn't been a blockbuster so far. "I learned financial services people are cynical. It was tough," Holtzman says. Still, he says, "the finance people like it because they hate the marketing people." He also went after the movie and the consumer products industries. Many marketers, Holtzman says, are terrified that the concept of "brand-stickiness" is going away. They fear that people aren't loyal to certain brands for their whole lives anymore, that the days of refusing to switch from Tide to Cheer are over.

"So this shows you the efficiency of your marketing dollars being spent?" asks Silver.

"Absolutely," says Holtzman. "Buzz seems to be a derivative of something," he says.

The talk turns to chat boards and how average people's comments are starting to become more powerful—a poster on a Web site like Raging Bull or Yahoo could influence investors just like financial analysts do.

"What do hedge funds use this for?" asks Silver.

"I was going to ask you," says Holtzman.

Berkeley, who is leaning so far back in his chair that the front two legs are off the ground and it looks like he'll fall over at any moment, says he'd like to use Opion's software at Nasdaq. "Let's screw around with this on a trial basis," he says. Holtzman nods. He says that for instance, SunTrust was a particularly hot Internet topic that day, having announced it would acquire Wachovia for $14.7 billion. "I've got a regulatory interest in that and an *interest* in that," says Berkeley, his southern accent coming through. Holtzman looks eager to hook up with Nasdaq. Silver suggests Opion talk to the Securities and Exchange Commission about a partnership.

As Holtzman talks, it's clear the company could go in many different directions at this moment. And any one of these comments could send it a particular way. Holtzman says he's staying away from making predictions based on the information because predictions are often wrong, and that could hurt Opion's young reputation. "But if you're not predictive, what good are you?" asks Ramsey.

"Why wouldn't you want to take your business and plug it directly into a hedge fund?" asks Morris, who's suggesting a hedge fund would pay big for proprietary access, or even to buy the system. Holtzman says sure, sounds good to him.

Holtzman says he has looked at the e-commerce marketers for potential deals.

"They're all wallpaper now," says Ramsey, dismissing the entire industry.

Berkeley starts talking about a service he currently subscribes to called Karma. It puts together graphs and research about whether a company's "karma" is good or not, information that potentially give clues about its uses and chance of survival.

"When do you need money?" asks Ramsey.

Holtzman says he'll run out in September and he's looking for strategic investors.

Berkeley suggests talking to a company called Cognos, where he was a board member for years. "And I want to follow up on this idea of buzz for Nasdaq companies," he says.

As the chocolate bars and crunchy Napoleons with apricot ginger sauce are finished, Holtzman departs. The members have been eyeing an arrangement of a couple dozen wine bottles on a backboard at the side of the room. Sachs explains that Kataria has sent over some wine for the members. She has attached personal notes to the gifts and copies of a recent article about her company. The multimillionaires leave Citronelle with a bottle in each hand, and they step out into the still-warm summer night, some to join Warner at the Majestic.

THE PORTFOLIO

D AVE H OLTZMAN got his first inkling one evening that things were about to get very bad when he was checking out the Web site of New Enterprise Associates, his start-up's biggest-name funder. He noticed that the photograph of Art Marks, the NEA venture capitalist who sat on Holtzman's board, was missing.

Marks was one of Holtzman's biggest fans, investing in his company Opion and bringing him to the Capital Investors, who also put money into the Internet "buzz" measuring business. The investor who chooses an investment and who sits on the company's board is that firm's protector. Without that person, the entrepreneur is on his own. "I know this isn't a nice analogy, but it's like pimps and streetwalkers," says Holtzman.

Holtzman soon learned that Marks had a disagreement with some of the other members of NEA, and he had left the firm as a result. NEA did not put another venture capitalist on Opion's board, basically sending the message to Holtzman and any potential future funders that Opion had been written off. In the venture capital world, when a company's current funders give up on the company, especially if they are as established as NEA, no other VC is likely to touch the deal. If NEA wasn't continuing to support Opion, there must be something wrong with it.

"It was the kiss of death for me," says Holtzman. "I became verboten." Actually there was something wrong with Opion—it hadn't attracted customers and revenues to keep the company going. But Holtzman says if he'd been able to raise more money, everything could have been different.

Holtzman's father died after a long illness the same week he had to shut the company down. As he laid off the rest of what once was forty employees through phone calls from Pittsburgh, where the funeral was held, Holtzman was struck by how many of the same words are used for the failing health of people and companies: triage, life support, near-death. "There was an odd sort of symmetry," he says.

By the end of 2001, five of the businesses in the Capital Investors eighteen-company portfolio, including Opion, had gone under. Others were officially alive but their owners were desperately trying to sell what was left of the company. Phone numbers were disconnected and placeholder Web sites didn't lead to anything beyond the home page. Not one of the portfolio companies had given the members any return on their investment. A return would require a "liquidity event," either a public offering or, much more likely in this market, a merger or sale.

The demise of the portfolio companies showed how the Capital Investors' through the club have done much more to help themselves and one another than the entrepreneurs who received their money. It was not a secret, though, that they thought of themselves first as a social group and only secondarily an investment club.

Still, this was a typical early-stage technology fund portfolio, circa 2001. "People don't make decisions during uncertain times," said a glum Eric Daniels, chief executive of portfolio company Zona Financiera, a financial Web site, a few days before shutting down the company.

Two years before, in the headiest of times, Reggie Aggarwal would ring a bell whenever Cvent snagged a new employee. Now, the bell rings when they get a customer. And the staff has been cut from one hundred at its height to thirty-five.

From his Arlington office, Aggarwal points to where he saw the smoke coming from the September 11 attack on the Pentagon. He sat at his desk that day directing event cancellations through Cvent's service, including a Mark Warner fund-raiser scheduled that night at 11600 Sunrise. Then he sent his workers home. When he told his salespeople to start calling again the Monday after the attacks, people who answered those calls yelled at his workers for being insensitive.

The Cvent offices, full of non-descript beige cubicles, are even on a normal day less than half full. "This used to be the quarter tour, now it's the dime tour," says Aggarwal, thirty-two.

"Hope we're not getting down to the nickel tour." There is some positive, though bittersweet, news today. Aggarwal's real-estate agent has finally found someone to take over half of the space: The government will set up grief counseling for Pentagon attack survivors. They will share Cvent's telephone system. Aggarwal was the archetypal start-up CEO. He put $300,000 on twelve credit cards to start the company after leaving a safe job as a corporate lawyer. At least three times he was within days of not meeting payroll. "I have a lot of pressure on me," says Aggarwal. "In two years we've seen a business cycle of fifteen to twenty years. I've been to hell and back."

But Aggarwal was brilliant at getting people to sign on to his dream, and he particularly concentrated on the Capital Investors, who were the most experienced and richest in the region. Aggarwal, who still lives at home with his parents, got to know most of the Capital Investors by reading about them in the newspaper and cold-calling them repeatedly until they answered. First, he interested them by starting a council for Indians in high-tech, a networking group that attracted high-level investors and executives by portraying itself as an exclusive gathering, just as many of the other groups were turning into mob scenes.

Aggarwal, who talks speedily and incessantly—he says if he gets a headache he just starts talking and it goes away—was the pied piper of Washington technology. Melton, Mandl, McDonnell, and Kim are personal investors in Cvent. Warner, Nasdaq,

Friedman Billings Ramsey Group, Inc., and Loudcloud are customers. MicroStrategy is an investor and a customer. Saylor's co-founder, the greatly overshadowed—for better or for worse—Sanju Bansal, has personally invested $2.8 million in Cvent. But does all his networking expertise and big-picture thinking translate into running a good business? It's not exactly what his investors concentrate on these days.

"No one cares about vision anymore," complains Aggarwal. "They care about burn rate and sales. It's like running a dry-cleaning shop."

Aggarwal says the worst moment for him was standing before the Capital Investors updating them on the company's problems. He felt like he'd failed the group. "I've never been beaten up harder in my life," he says. But he was also disappointed in them, too. Aggarwal thinks the members should at least have ended the evening with an encouraging thought. "These icons scolded me. I felt like I let them down."

The group didn't break its rule by investing in a second round in Cvent. So the next morning, Aggarwal hit the phones, begging every individual investor who already had money in the company to re-invest. With hours to spare, he managed to scrape together the cash, some from new Capital Investor Ed Mathias of The Carlyle Group and some, even, from Global Internet Ventures, the international fund run by Bill Melton and Jeong Kim.

"They own me," says Aggarwal. "They own me for life.

They've made my dream come true." He pauses. "At least up to this point."

There were really several reasons a company would want a Capital Investors investment. The money, of course, was one, but it was rarely the most important, and usually a relatively small amount. The idealistic among the start-up executives wanted a combination of validation and criticism from those in the group they admired.

"I had never presented a business plan before a group of people before," said Dr. D'Orta with the defibrillator business. "Ever." He said Saylor's questions, especially, were "disarming," but that he felt it was a sanity check for his business from people who knew better than himself.

Bruce Mancinelli, founder of online survey company Web-Surveyor, says he showed up to see if he had a dumb idea. He had seen the movie *Gladiator* the week before his presentation and said he couldn't help thinking about that bloody mess as he was standing in front of the group at The Palm in Tysons Corner. "I thought it was a horrible way to evaluate a company," said Mancinelli. "They don't look at the numbers. It's 'Did you capture someone's fancy?'" Still, the $300,000 he received from the group turned WebSurveyor from an idea into a real company, and he's grateful for that.

Depending on what night they presented, the person the entrepreneur most wanted to meet may not have shown up. That was a problem, because besides money and validation, many of the presenters were there for the connections. Some portfolio companies wanted Steve Case at AOL, Jeong Kim at Lucent, and John Sidgmore at WorldCom to introduce them to the right person at their respective firms. Others didn't so much concentrate on that specific introduction. They just wanted to list those names on their press releases, particularly Case and Andreessen, and see where that got them.

Keith Wardell, CEO of Shop2U, did eventually get to AOL through the group and negotiated to be their email marketer, meaning Shop2U would send email advertisements to AOL users. Problem was, AOL asked to be paid $9 million over a year-and-a-half to two-year period for the honor. "When AOL wants you to be their provider, they want you to pay for it," says Wardell. Shop2U couldn't raise the money; they didn't do a deal. Shop2U does have customers like 1-800-Flowers and TravelSmith, who pay them.

Wardell says that since he is in his fifties, he probably wasn't as nervous as some of the younger presenters, even though the room where he gave his pitch had a glass wall that looked out into the main room of the restaurant. He felt like 200 people watched his presentation, including the chefs, who stopped to listen. In January of 2001, Shop2U cut a third of their employees, down to about twenty-two.

Sean Milliken is younger and does admit he was nervous presenting his company MissionFish, an online auction benefiting nonprofits that did snag $100,000 from the group. That evening at Cafe Milano in Georgetown, Case asked him the question everyone asks: "Why wouldn't eBay just do this?" Milliken says it was "very surreal" talking to Case about his plans. Still, investment from the group was MissionFish's first big break. Milliken moved his company from Atlanta to Washington because Capital Investors only invests in Washington-area companies.

At first, the connections through Capital Investors helped companies get meetings with other investors. Just saying they were on the list made them more attractive. It became less important as there was a plethora of seed capital. When after the crash again came a capital drought, the group as early-stage investors were once again relevant. And it became easier for the group to get better valuations on deals, meaning more of the company for less money.

But a criticism both sides are aware of is that once the money is invested, unless the entrepreneur has relationships with specific individuals in the group, they tend to be fending for themselves. Sachs says he's trying to work on "wish lists" where companies outline which deals and hires they need to grow and who they want to meet.

It was surprising to see how disinterested the group members were in both their investment—if this had been a typical venture fund they would have been much more involved in each deal—and in their roles as potential mentors to the entrepreneurs. The fund was to be a hybrid of investing for profit and encouragement, but after the initial investment, little was seen of either.

"Where we've fallen down with the companies is we haven't provided the kind of mentoring we should," says McDonnell.

And this after all, was one of the original goals of the group: To help the next generation. Along the way, the mission blurred. Part of the problem, certainly, was that it is difficult for members of the group to bet on ideas they know won't work, even if they like the entrepreneur.

Mancinelli vacillates between lauding the group and beating it up. He says he was shocked that after the dinner, even though the group invested, he could never convince any of the members to help him out. He was also disappointed that the portfolio companies were never even introduced to one another. Mancinelli was hoping there would be at least one event where the CEOs of each company could gather together. But there was no "cross-pollination." "It's the who's who of mega-naires," he says about the club. "It looks great on paper but you don't have reach to those people."

But then Mancinelli tries to consider what the investment has done for him. He's attempting to be more realistic about his expectations. And they did give him money. "They fill an absolute crying need," he says. "It provides an opportunity for the seed to be planted. That's all."

Holtzman says in the end some time and advice from the members would have been worth more than the money.

Aggarwal thinks it would be strange and somewhat unseemly to call one of them for help while their own company was falling apart. "They've got their own set of problems," shrugged Aggarwal. "It's hard for them to help us. Even though I'm Mr. Networker, I don't want to call in my favors until it really matters. These are people I want to know for thirty years."

Webversa chief executive Tom Lewis isn't so understanding. Lewis is trying to keep his company alive and needs all the help he can get. He's furious at the Capital Investors because he basically hasn't heard from them since he got their money. "It pisses me off," says Lewis. "Just pick up the phone. Hello?"

Lewis says he requested introductions at some of the companies the members run. No luck. "It's a bit of a bait-and-switch type thing," he says. It's also a problem, as he's looking for new financing, to explain why Capital Investors won't be in on this round. "I don't think they care. It's 'By the way, we left a little tip on the table.' Dinner money."

At almost every Capital Investor meeting, there is discussion and sometimes argument about what kinds of investments the group should make. Some believe in the three-guys-in-a-basement model. Others think that especially in a struggling economy, more proven technologies are the way to go. A few like betting on the person presenting, while others favor replacing the CEO as long as the idea is good. One faction within the group actually proposed switching all new investments to nonprofits. The joke is, well, most of them are nonprofitable now. But that idea didn't fly.

Jonathan Silver, who runs venture capital firm Core Capital, says it's not exactly the methodology he's used to. His firm takes about six and a half months to decide on an investment; the Capital Investors averages eight minutes.

Ed Mathias says one of the group members' wives said to him she's sick of these $200,000 dinners. But otherwise, no one seems to complain about the losses too much. Mathias also looks at the investments this way: If he likes the entrepreneur, it may be his second or third start-up that works. And Mathias wants to be around for the "rebound" investment.

While the Capital Investors clearly focuses more on the social aspects of the club, one might think that the person in charge of finding the deals and managing the fund, a twenty-something still paying off his wife's student loan, would not so easily brush off a failing portfolio.

Sachs says he struggles with it. But he's in this, too, more for the networking, to meet people who will take him to his next career, rather than for the money. "This is the peak of my notoriety," he says, noting he talks to anyone and everyone in the technology community. His calls are returned. His own next thing will be a step up, he hopes, with maybe fewer bosses.

Sachs is holding on to hope especially for Viztec, and has even joined the company's board. "I'm baby-sitting fifty-year-olds," he says. "It's sad but true." Sachs makes $100,000 a year, plus a $20,000 bonus in June. And he's got equal equity stake to all the members, without having put up any money. If things don't turn around, Sachs just may be the only member to make money from the club.

However, the members are constantly, and successfully, fund-raising one another, the largest projects so far being Morino's venture philanthropy fund, Ramsey's investment fund, and of course, Warner's campaign. The group in total gave $1.2 million in personal contributions to their friend, many in the $100,000 range. Warner himself ended up spending $5 million on the race. So quite a nice chunk—$6.2 million—of Warner's total $20-million record campaign war chest came directly from the pockets of the members of the dinner club.

CHAPTER THIRTEEN

TEATRO GOLDONI, WASHINGTON, D.C.

November 2001

THIS NIGHT, UNDER THE LOW LIGHTS that illuminate the bright gold and blue harlequin patterns on the walls of Teatro Goldoni, there is a mixture of alternating somberness and joy of the kind usually reserved for weddings and funerals.

Two months and one day after the tragedies of September 11, still reeling from unfamiliar terror that manifested itself in hijackings and poisoned letters, this morning another plane has gone down in New York, killing nearly 300 people. It is a horrible day.

But it is also the first time many of the Capital Investors have seen one another since their candidate, the one who the group collectively buoyed with their money and votes, won the race for governor in Virginia. It is a wonderful day.

Teatro is the Italian word for theater, and Goldoni was an eighteenth-century playwright who loved food. The restaurant is set up as a series of stages. The Capital Investors gather on the top floor in a huge private room with a glass wall overlooking the kitchen where Venetian specialties are prepared, which overlooks the main dining room. A large square table with a white tablecloth, blue and yellow china, blue glass tea lights, and a white and green floral centerpiece is set up for the group.

"Our guy won!" says Walker enthusiastically as the Capital Investors begin to arrive and place their drink orders. Those members who weren't in Richmond for election night have seen newspaper photos and television clips of Warner's acceptance speech, many of which show Ramsey onstage immediately at Warner's right side. "Were you running, too?" Marks asks Ramsey.

Leonsis strides in, grins at everyone, and bows to Kimsey, grabbing his hand and kissing it. "What's next, locusts?" he asks the group. "Frogs?" suggests Kimsey.

Kimsey had recently toured Ground Zero in New York with Mayor Giuliani and Queen Noor. Kimsey doesn't like the word *dating,* but says yes, he is "spending time" with Queen Noor these days. The visit to the site of the World Trade Center attacks was more horrifying than he'd expected. "I've done two tours in Vietnam," says Kimsey. "I've seen a lot of shit in my life and I wasn't prepared. It was sixteen acres of devastation. You can hear thousands of souls screaming out of that hole." One of the saddest things he saw were writings and carvings on a wood platform where family members were brought to look at the wreckage.

Leonsis says Kimsey owes him big-time. Colombian President Andres Pastrana was in Washington the week before and mentioned to his friend Kimsey that Michael Jordan was one of his all-time heroes. Pastrana said he would like to go to a game and meet Jordan. So Kimsey called Leonsis, who set about securing the nine seats (eight for bodyguards) the president would require in the owners' box. The day of the game, Leonsis received word that Pastrana instead had to be in New York that day, never mind.

Many of the members seem to think today's new tragedy has the marks of terrorism. Several of them talk about one circulating theory that the plane was headed for the United Nations.

"The coincidences are too many," says Marks.

As the members take their seats, Ramsey clinks a wineglass with his knife. It's time to talk about the good news. Warner is not here tonight, but on his way back from a brief vacation in Puerto Rico with his wife following the election.

"Was Mark happy?" asks Marks.

"Is he ever happy?" replies Ramsey, who spent a full day the week before the election traveling with Warner, going to all the campaign stops and greeting as many voters as they could find. "He probably enjoyed it for about an hour."

"Mark sends his sincere thanks to this group," says Ramsey. Then he shakes his head. "He's got an enormous job ahead of him."

Silver, who worked for the Clinton administration, says Warner's method of appealing to both political parties while somehow not alienating one or the other will give him more power. "Mark just developed a national profile," says Silver. "He didn't win as a Democrat or a Republican."

Walker seems skeptical. "Let's hope that's true," he says.

Marks points out that Warner's opponent, Mark Earley, did a great job of sounding like a Democrat by his persistent criticism of Warner's wealth. Walker and Melton joke about the others who didn't get the "memo." They both have new grayish-white beards. As long as their wives like it, it stays.

Sachs leads Michael Rosenbaum, chief executive of Catalyst Solutions, to the room. Rosenbaum, a short young man with dark hair, a dark suit, and a somewhat hysterical laugh, is Harvard undergrad and Harvard law. He worked in the Clinton White House as an economist on technology and urban issues; this is his first start-up.

Catalyst has developed software that screens and trains job-hunters, and then places that person in the right position. Rosenbaum is looking for a $1-million investment round.

The members eat bread dipped in olive oil and marinated olives as Rosenbaum begins his speech. He tries to stay out of the way of the waiter, apologizing once for bumping into him as the server goes around to each Capital Investor, taking dinner orders.

Greenfield and new member Ed Mathias, a venture capitalist with The Carlyle Group, begin peppering Rosenbaum with questions. Burton asks Rosenbaum to explain the company's current contracts, which he does, earnestly.

"It's like AmericaWorks then?" asks Silver.

"Right," says Rosenbaum.

The concept of training displaced workers to do something new is appealing, especially in these times. "What about venture capitalists?" jokes Burton. "Give me a call," laughs Rosenbaum. Then Burton, who is from Boston and went to Boston College, says to the members sitting closest to him that whenever he sees two Harvards on a resume, a flag goes up.

Silver says regardless of what the group decides, Rosenbaum should talk to a person he knows who could help. Silver searches for a phone number on his BlackBerry. "Got a pen?" asks Ramsey, trying to move things along, as Rosenbaum pulls one out and scribbles a name and number on his presentation.

The kitchen, one stage below and now preparing the members' lamb chops and grouper filets, is getting noisier, drowning out some of the conversation. "Do you have highly proprietary psychological testing and where does that come from?" asks Burton.

Morino quickly follows up, asking who in the management group has experience in this industry. As the sautéed calamari is served in small white square dishes, the other Catalyst executive who had been standing next to Rosenbaum begins to talk about his work at Sylvan Learning Systems. Morino is not impressed. "Help me with this," he says. "Their record has been abysmal. Abysmal is polite."

Mathias asks if the executives are paying themselves. "Yes," says Rosenbaum. "Not as much as we would make at a law firm."

"What is driving you to do this and what do you want the company to become?" asks Mathias. Rosenbaum emits a bit of nervous laughter, and says: "To offer people opportunities they otherwise might not have." He pauses, as if he's unsure whether to say the next statement, but then continues on. "My grandfather escaped from Nazi Germany in the 1930s. There were economic dislocations. If we can solve economic dislocations . . ."

Marks, Fernandez, and Morino continue on a combination questioning/advice-giving roll. And then Sachs walks over, time is up. He leads them downstairs.

"Tough room, huh?" asks Leonsis. "Piranhas," says Fernandez. "But that was kind."

"We've always been very astute in our investments," says Burton, continuing the running joke that none of the portfolio companies has so far returned any money to the members. "There's very little leverage here, but it's a noble cause," Burton adds.

"The kid was blowing smoke," says Morino, about the second executive.

Well, says Sachs, guess that's a no.

"Who brought this in?" asks Kim, who was silent through the presentation. Kim hasn't been to a meeting in a long time and seems surprised at the choice.

"I did, and I think it could be a profitable company," says Sachs.

As the raspberry sorbet and chocolate cake are served, Leonsis regales the group with stories about Warner Bros.' future movie-making plans—a laundry list of super-hero sequels. The group breaks up for the evening, with Leonsis, Fernandez, and Kim walking down to a banquette in the main dining room for after-dinner drinks. Despite a losing streak for both the Capitals and the Wizards, even with Michael Jordan playing, Leonsis and Fernandez are upbeat. They have recently added AOL executive Jack Davies, OTG Software chief executive Rick Kay, and investment banker George Stamas to their owner's circle, spots that opened up after investor Jonathan Ledecky sold his shares back to Leonsis. Lincoln Holdings wants Kim next. Others in the group quiz Ramsey on Mark Warner's state of mind, what the election party was like, and how he's emotionally handling the win.

Silver is thinking about these new projects of the Capital Investors and how they are influencing what will be the next Washington. "It's a new generation," he says, looking around the table.

CHAPTER FOURTEEN

THE ELECTION

OR FIFTY-THREE YEARS, the unofficial kickoff of the Virginia governor's race has been held in a one-stoplight town called Wakefield, Virginia. The event is affectionately called the shad planking, or simply "The Shad." Thousands of Virginians come out to drink beer, eat shad—a bottom-dwelling bony fish slow-roasted over a fire—and do some country-style politicking.

As the Democratic candidate, Mark Warner, forty-six, all height and teeth and handshakes, strides through the crowd on this chilly April day, a few words echo through the crowd, almost like a chorus. They are "millionaire," "rich," and "wealthy." Most of the people out today, a predominantly male group (women have only been invited in recent years), many in camouflage and baseball hats and some with Confederate flag stickers on their vests, know only one thing about Warner. They might not know how he got it, but they understand he has money. Warner's campaign slogan in Wakefield, a town in Southern Virginia about three hours from Washington, might as well be, "Don't hate me because I'm rich."

Republican opponent Mark Earley has chosen money as the cornerstone of his argument against Warner. This election would become the most expensive the state had ever seen, with Warner raising $20 million for his coffers and Earley $11 million for his own treasury. By the end, Warner will have put $5 million into his own campaign.

When it comes time for the candidates to speak, they gather up on a podium where the opening act consists of piped-in songs that croon "Mama, don't let your babies grow up to be cowboys," and "Looking for love in all the wrong places."

As the audience stands surrounded by tall pine trees, eating smoked shad from paper plates, Warner is pummeled for his financial success.

Earley's insults are a riff designed to appeal to the working class, especially toward those who are distrustful and a bit envious of the rich.

"It's an honor to share the platform with my wealthy, I mean, worthy, opponent."

"Mark, I'd be here earlier but I got held up by your thirty-car motorcade."

And a couple of myth-busters.

"It's not true that if elected, Mark has promised that next year it'll be the prime rib planking."

"It's not true that he calls the governor's mansion a nice little getaway."

Warner's not exactly in Northern Virginia anymore. But

he's trying to fit in. He's sponsoring a NASCAR race car and will be turkey-hunting with an influential potential supporter. The transformation from Limo Warner to NASCAR Warner happens quickly and easily. Beginning twenty miles away from the shad planking, Warner's presence is felt. Multitudes of Warner signs start popping up, dwarfing Hager and Earley signs. They don't let up, leading directly inside the event grounds. Warner's campaign staff put up 15,000 signs for the occasion, working through the night to make sure the signs would guide the voter right into the Warner booth where they would be handed a Budweiser. Like many politicians, Warner's got a young, idealistic staff who will give up their outside lives for at least a year to try to get their candidate elected. One staffer fell asleep at the wheel sometime after midnight on his way from Washington to Wakefield. He crashed into a median, somehow escaped with a few scratches, and showed up on time for The Shad. Another young staffer was stopped by a state trooper on her way to the event, doing seventy-two in a fifty-five zone. She didn't want to miss Cooter.

Cooter, really, is at the nexus of politics and old Virginia. His real name is Ben Jones, and he's both a former Democratic Georgia congressman (he eventually lost to Newt Gingrich) and the actor who played car mechanic Cooter Davenport in the television show *The Dukes of Hazzard.* These days, Jones runs Cooter's Place, a barbecue joint/shrine to the show in Sperryville, Virginia. Cooter is the celebrity of The Shad, and Warner's got him.

After seeing the thousands of signs along the way, the shad-goer is next met at the ticket entrance ($14 for all you can eat, which includes fried shad roe, a kibble-like food served on a little paper tray) by the sticker-people. They are recruiting for their team, and they paper anyone they can with campaign stickers, on their back if they don't look out. Some people walk around eating their roe plastered with more badges than an Eagle Scout.

The Warner booth is immediately to the right of the entrance, a great location. The prime attraction is the huge beer truck with the Warner insignia, serving free Budweiser and Bud Light. There's also a great, real bluegrass band, called The Bluegrass Brothers.

One of Warner's supporters, Mudcat Saunders, wrote lyrics for a twangy Warner campaign song to the tune of an old ditty that was often played on *The Andy Griffith Show.*

"No more tricks in politics that leave our future grim," sings the band. That's Saunders's favorite line. Saunders says the song is a "message of hope." With the music and the beer, the Warner booth is a hit. As the candidate walks in, he is surrounded by swarms of people who want to ask him a question, get their picture taken with him, or just take a look at the guy. When television reporters near, including a CNN reporter who looks out of place in a suit, Warner's staffers surround him with signs, forming an instant backdrop for any photo-op. Warner is expressive, telling stories, cocking his head to one side, leaning in, listening, nodding, and flashing huge elect-me smiles.

His "driver" Edward, a twenty-something who is the son of one of Warner's Alexandria neighbors, is stuck to him like glue. Edward tapes the interviews, the constituent questions, and the random chit-chat with a micro-cassette recorder. He takes down names and numbers of people who want to follow up. In a fleece vest with a water bottle stuck in his back pocket, Edward looks in control but slightly worried as he guides Warner through the masses. He can never look away from his charge. Warner does not look over people's shoulders as he's talking to them. If the person's taking up too much time, Edward will intervene, but Warner will not be the rude one.

In khakis, a blue shirt, and tan tie and carrying a blue blazer, Warner is pretty much in the candidate uniform for such an event. It's a different crowd than his city friends.

In this fifty-third year, one tradition has changed. For the first time all gubernatorial candidates are invited to speak, while previous years only an already-elected official took the podium. So this year campaign speeches interrupt the drink and conversation. The candidates are careful not to get too heavy in this laid-back atmosphere and mainly stick to jokes during their speech time.

Up on the stage, Democrats are seated on one side and Republicans on the other. Earley's camp has trotted out Republican Senator John Warner, who a few years before beat Mark Warner in the senate race.

Warner is introduced with the boast that he's helped found

more than fifty technology firms. Warner says he's been to many a shad, but never as a speaker. "It makes me feel like Zsa Zsa Gabor's eighth husband. I know what to do but I don't know how to make it exciting," Warner says. Many members of the crowd immediately look over at John Warner, who of course, was one of Elizabeth Taylor's seven husbands. "I'm not touching that one," says Mark Warner.

Those who remembered the Warner vs. Warner race might also recall that Mark Warner spent $10 million of his own money in an attempt to win the senate seat. His critics bring up that number now, saying elections just can't be bought, although it's easier to try in Virginia, where the state has no limits to how much money individuals or corporations give to a candidate or campaign. Warner would start this race with an estimated $200-million personal fortune, and a cadre of friends willing to put up whatever it took.

"The boys" as Warner calls his fellow Capital Investors, are some of Warner's top supporters, with twenty-one of the twenty-six (including Warner himself) donating to the campaign, according to the Virginia Public Access Project, which tracks political donations. Even Maryland residents like Marks and Sidgmore and Republicans Fernandez and Mandl ponied up. Fernandez, who worked for Jack Kemp and gave a prime-time speech at the 2000 Republican presidential convention, said he was told that his donation to Warner meant he wouldn't be considered for an advisory panel in the Bush administration.

"I'm a Republican but I'm investing in Mark," says Green-field. "The Democrats and the Republicans are saying 90 percent of the same things."

It annoys Warner's supporters, like Susan DeFife, a Virginia businesswoman who saw her first start-up fail (a company that was rejected for investment by the Capital Investors) and her second sold, that Earley is concentrating on his opponent's wealth.

"It's the American dream," says DeFife, a Republican who says she'll vote for Warner and has donated to his campaign. "That's what we're *supposed* to be doing. Why are we bashing the guy for that?"

As a young man, Warner seemed headed toward the life of an attorney. He went to George Washington University and then Harvard Law School. But way before the Internet craze, Warner had another unusual burst of luck that he recognized as opportunity. When the government was giving away chunks of wireless spectrum in the early 1980s, few people could imagine the promise of cellular phones. But Warner and a few colleagues fashioned themselves as cellular license brokers, scooped up as much spectrum as they could get, and made millions in the process. Later, Warner co-founded Columbia Capital, an investment firm in Alexandria, so he could bet on many companies at once.

The wireless world aside, Warner has always had a taste for politics. He is, like many politicians, charismatic but a pleaser, the kind of person who seems to change to fit the situation he's in and the people he's with at the same time. His easy transformation made many wonder who he really was. He seemed to be on many sides of an issue, trying to convince everyone from the gay rights activists to the Confederate flag supporters that he would be the best governor for them.

During the gubernatorial race, the Republican Party of Virginia set up a web site at www.whichwarner.com, dedicated to the "changing face of Mark Warner." The site pits Warner against himself in numerous issues, from welfare reform to Virginia's car tax. The site features a picture of Warner with a cartoonish bubble above his head, saying, "I can provide business leadership . . . because I caught a lucky break with the cell phone boom."

Although Warner became better known in the 1990s for his corporate side, he long had his hand in the political realm, where he was as comfortable as anywhere else, and certainly did not drop naïvely into the 2001 governor's race without knowing his way around the political system. Warner managed Douglas Wilder's successful run for governor of Virginia in 1989, then he chaired the Democratic Party of Virginia from 1993 to 1995. He became an adept fund-raiser, and many said that everything he accomplished in business—the connections, the money— were aimed methodically toward the big race ahead.

Keith Frederick, Warner's college roommate at George Washington University, occasionally travels with Warner on the campaign trail. Frederick says he and Warner were influenced by the Kennedy "call to action," and that is what drives Warner to want something more than money. "We were behind the hippies but before the Reagan conservatives," Frederick says of their generation.

The list of Warner's top fifteen technology and finance contributors shows clearly how his business friendships are helping him in the political arena. In fact, it looks like an attendance rundown for the club, plus a few other familiar faces. Eight of the fifteen are his inner circle, members of the Capital Investors.

Art Marks, who gave $102,500, was Warner's top donor from the technology or finance community, according to the Virginia Public Access Project. Melton, Fernandez, Morino, Kimsey, and Leonsis each gave $100,000; Ramsey donated $75,000; and Saylor $60,000; according to the group.

Three of Warner's partners at Columbia Capital—James Murray, Mark Kington, and David Mixer—also made the list. Eric Billings and Emanuel Friedman, the two men who founded FBR—where Warner held a board seat—were also top donors.

But while the biggest bucks were coming from his club friends, Warner was also attracting money outside that circle. By the end of the race, he had accepted donations from 15,000 individuals, also a record for Virginia elections. His friends see the fund-raising as all part of the expensive business of politics.

"It's a multimillion dollar start-up with a one-day selling season," says Ramsey. "You either succeed or you fail."

Building his friend network and creating a financial support network were one and the same. Warner began this campaign with a net knit of dollars and influence firmly in place. While he was helping create Capital Investors, he also set up four venture capital funds in different areas of Virginia: Richmond, Southside, Southwest, and Hampton Roads. Warner invested about $250,000 in each. But instead of simply putting his own money into these pools he brought in leaders of each of those areas, with about 300 total joining the four funds. It was clear that the creation of the funds was, at least in part, politically motivated. His Northern Virginia friends laughed at the idea that there could be good deals way out there. It's too early to judge the financial success of the funds, but right now they look like most venture capital funds that invested heavily in high-tech—losing some companies and trying to keep the rest alive.

But the creation of the rural venture capital funds shows that if nothing else, Warner knows how to get a group of people to gather around the common goal of making money. He may be impatient and inexperienced, having never before held an elected office. But he has an uncanny ability to rally people around what drives them—and is even better at it when the motivation is economic.

As a partner at Columbia, Warner has had hits and misses. A great success was providing the initial capital to wireless company Nextel in 1987, which had been named Fleet Call. There were failures like SpaceWorks and Capital Investors portfolio company Zona Financiera, which went out of business, but other interesting and potentially lucrative investments like XM Satellite Radio, which went public in 1999, and Torrent Networking Technologies, which was acquired by Ericsson, also in 1999. A venture capitalist can ride a long while on one or two blockbuster deals.

Through these investments, Warner became a fixture in the Washington area business community. Still, there was at least one Northern Virginia contingent not likely to choose Warner—the Fairfax, Virginia–based National Rifle Association. Warner courted the NRA, meeting with its representatives, and saying he supported the right to hunt and fish. But he also said he would veto any bill that would repeal the state's law that limits handgun purchases to one a month, a top issue for the NRA. But Warner changed his position on another important gun issue. During the first gubernatorial debate, he said he would not support banning guns at Fairfax County recreation centers. A few weeks later, Warner reversed that stance, saying he in fact would sign a law banning guns from Fairfax County recreation centers. Before the election, the NRA made the unusual move of not endorsing either candidate, considered by some a vote for Warner.

But not everyone liked Warner's centrist, pleasing-everyone campaign. The Brady Campaign to Prevent Gun Violence harshly criticized Warner for seeking the NRA's nod. "Warner seems to think that he can 'have his cake and eat it, too' but trying to play both sides of the fence on this critical life and death issue is disingenuous, and it is dangerous political gamesmanship," said Michael Barnes, president of the Brady Campaign, in a statement.

The next morning after The Shad, Warner will go turkeyhunting for the first time in his life. An influential Virginia couple wants to get to know the candidate better. And in these parts, you don't invite him to dinner. You invite him hunting at the crack of dawn. Warner's staff has prepared a memo detailing the art of killing fowl, along with various hunting tips, and placed it in his daily schedule book. The book tells him what kind of crowd to expect at the event, gives the history of The Shad, and reminds him who to thank for donations and introductions.

A few months earlier, Warner had the same toothy smile and easy attitude at a fund-raiser for the tech elite at eCiti Cafe, a converted warehouse turned nightclub in Tysons Corner that caters to the high-tech crowd. Some of the Capital Investors are there, including Saylor and Ramsey. Warner's partners at Columbia Capital, Karl Khoury and Jane Dietz, young venture capitalists, joked about the continual fund-raising shakedown by their colleague. Former Clinton press secretary Mike McCurry is there, too, having recently joined the tech world as CEO of Grassroots.com.

This was only one of a series of "birthday fund-raisers" where Warner grows a year older again and again, but stays the same age, a political Rip Van Winkle. At eCiti, Russ Ramsey's wife, Norma, a beautiful blonde woman who is known for her charity work in Washington, takes the microphone and sings in a breathy voice, "Happy birthday, Mr. Governor."

Warner talks tech to this crowd, saying it's why he wants this office at this time. "The reason I want to run for governor is that we are at a moment of historical transformation," he says. Warner boasts that he's out-raised his Republican opponents two to one, but well, you can never have enough. On the way out, a huge cobalt-blue bowl sits on a table, waiting for little envelopes to be deposited, full of new donations.

Of all the members in the club, Warner and Ramsey are among the closest personal friends. Their children are playmates; they go on vacations together. They met in 1994 when they joined the same group that was trying to bring a professional baseball team to Virginia. They had both graduated from George Washington University, and Warner, who was on the university's board, recruited Ramsey to join him.

Although Ramsey has a framed picture of President Bush on his desk along with portraits of his wife, his two red-haired sons, and his little blonde daughter, he says he doesn't consider himself Republican or Democrat. He does consider himself for Warner but doesn't envy him the race.

"He's got one of the worst jobs in America running for governor. He's always on," says Ramsey. Not that it surprises Ramsey that he's running. While Warner made his mark in

technology business, he has coveted elected office since child-
hood.

"He's had the political disease since he was six," says Ramsey, who thinks Warner considers this the ultimate challenge.
"He's suffering from divine dissatisfaction, which is a blessing
and a curse," says Ramsey.

When he was thinking about running, Warner asked Bill
Gorog, the eldest Capital Investor, for his opinion. Gorog
advised against it, saying the life of a candidate, and more so the
life of a politician, can wreak havoc on a family. It's just not
worth the power, he said.

Angel investing expert Cal Simmons, who held a fund-
raiser for Warner at his house, watched the transformation of
his friend to public figure. "It's easier being a faceless businessman," Simmons says.

Warner himself is exhausted on the trail. When asked about
other subjects, he's out of the loop. "All my oxygen's being
sucked out by politics," he sighs. "It's all-consuming."

And as Earley constantly pointed out, the one with the most
money at the end might not be the winner. Earley's campaign
focused on his political experience and his opponent's lack of it.
Still, Earley needed to raise some cash and was also looking to
attract the business people of Northern Virginia.

In June, it looked like it would be a bad moment in the
Warner campaign when Earley cheerfully announced he landed
seventy financial supporters from the Northern Virginia busi-

ness community, the area Warner had seemed to own. But the joy in Earley's camp quickly dissipated as questions arose about one donor, Thruport Technologies chairman Bruce Waldack, and his relationship to the Internet pornography industry. It turned out that Thruport had sold a software system to a site called Sex.com. Earley, a Christian conservative, had supported restrictions on minors' access to online pornography. Earley eventually returned the $47,000 Waldack had donated.

When it came to donations and money spent on television ads, it did seem the race had much to do with money.

Earley said he would spend $400,000 for a series of television ads over three weeks. But Warner would pay out $500,000 every week through November 6.

As the Warner–Earley debates began, it was clear Earley would not just focus on money, but on the attitude many of the tech rich have, that if they are successful in business, they will be successful in other realms as well. It is an attitude embraced on one hand by those who like the thought of fresh insights, but mocked by those who think it is pure arrogance.

"I would never in a million years go up to my opponent's place of business . . . and say, 'Hire me to lead your venture capital fund because I've got a lot of new ideas,'" said Earley at the first debate held on July 14 in White Sulphur Springs, West Virginia.

Warner fought back by constantly pointing to the Republican's inability to pass a state budget that year. "In business, you'd be out of business," he said.

The race switched traditional party roles as Earley continued to rail against capitalism and Warner courted gun owners.
While Warner featured a gun and a fishing pole on a bright
orange *Sportsmen for Warner* bumper sticker, a slogan of Earley's was "Vote for the Mark with the mortgage."

And the money-bashing continued. On a WTOP radio
address, Governor James S. Gilmore III (R) lambasted Warner
as a "really rich guy" who has "basically declared he's going to
try to buy the race."

While most of high-tech Washington found headquarters in
the Tysons, Reston, Herndon area, Warner kept his offices near his
home in the historic Old Town section of Alexandria. Columbia
Capital and MRW Enterprises, Warner's personal office, have
space overlooking the water, a location where there is a briny
smell in the air many days. A permanent fixture in the offices is
Nicholas Perrins, the head of MRW Enterprises. Perrins, tall,
skinny, and red-haired, is thirty-two, but looks to be in his twenties. He has been running Warner's financial life for ten years. He
began in the lowly "driver" position, but became Warner's most
trusted adviser, his chief of staff. Perrins's hand is in everything,
from venture capital investments to personal stakes in restaurants
and movie studios, and of course, the political side.

As Warner prepared to run, political Washington and tech
Washington began, slowly, to move closer. First, there were the
ex-politicians who joined tech boards and took stock options.
They wanted, like everyone else, to be on the cutting-edge and

to make some money in the process. Bob Dole joined Equal-Footing, a Capital Investors portfolio company. Jack Kemp was on Proxicom's board and Al Haig was a long-time member of AOL's board of directors. Colin Powell was also an AOL board member. Even Clinton press secretary Mike McCurry caught start-up fever, becoming the CEO of an online advocacy group. "I'm wearing myself out as a pundit," said McCurry. "I'm less and less interested in being a talking head.

"Doing a start-up has a lot of the feel and energy of a campaign," McCurry said enthusiastically when he started with the company. Like many Internet firms, the company has since taken off the *.com* in its name, and is now known as Grassroots Enterprise.

McCurry had talked to Steve Case in 1995 about taking over for Jean Villanueva (now Jean Case) who left AOL after Case and Villanueva announced they had a personal relationship. But that job never happened. McCurry doesn't like to estimate exactly how much he probably would have made in stock at AOL. AOL, in fact, almost exclusively hired people with political backgrounds to join its public relations and marketing team. Kathy Bushkin, who did take Jean Case's place, had been Gary Hart's press secretary. Others came from both sides of the fence: the Democratic National Committee, the Reagan White House, various congressional offices. And in fact, AOL was run much like a campaign, reacting quickly and quietly to crises and more loudly promoting successes.

And politics and tech intersected again when the Bush–Cheney team, still unofficial during the last days of ballot-counting, needed a transition office. They ended up in Dream-Labs, a McLean technology incubator that had lots of high-tech space and whose managers had a connection to Bush family friend Bobbie Kilberg, president of the Northern Virginia Technology Council.

The technology community rallied for both candidates on September 21, the first gubernatorial debate after the attacks on the World Trade Center and the Pentagon. The Fairfax Park Marriott was decked out in red, white, and blue, with little flags at each centerpiece and patriotic-colored balloons all over the packed hotel ballroom. Many of the men wore American flag ties and several women wore red, white, and blue pins on their lapels. The 600 people gathered for the lunch and debate were handed paper flags on their way out.

In their opening remarks, both candidates, wearing dark gray suits, white shirts, and red ties, paid respect to those who died and voiced quiet anger at terrorism.

But quickly, the debate moved on to issues of transportation, tax, and guns. "Things in politics have gotten topsy-turvy," admitted Warner as he came out to support some traditionally Republican causes and Earley repeatedly bashed Warner for making too much money.

The debate did return several times to a controversy caused by the attacks: the fate of Ronald Reagan National Airport, which is located in Virginia. The government was considering shutting down the airport permanently, and it remained closed at that point. Both candidates, again sounding similar on the issue, claimed they would reopen National airport, no matter what. But they didn't say why or how they would do it, nor did they speculate that it might have already opened by the time either would reach office. That much was still too uncertain.

The election was again overshadowed after the United States began attacks in Afghanistan in early October, forcing the cancellation of what was to be the final debate. This was good for Warner, who had performed badly in another televised debate. And it was also very good for Warner that President Bush, whose approval rating had been rising swiftly since the September 11 terrorism, spent little time supporting the Republican candidates in these off-year elections. Fund-raisers sponsored by Bush and Vice President Cheney were canceled. A couple of appearances of Bush with Earley on the campaign trail or even a taped endorsement could have really helped the Republican ticket, according to election-watchers.

About two weeks before election day, *The Washington Post* endorsed Warner, saying "We don't find the choice a difficult one." Polls showed him up to 10 percentage points ahead. But then, finally, just before the election, the Earley camp finally got a statement from President Bush supporting their candidate. They sent out hundreds of thousands of copies of the letter. A nod from the currently popular war-time President Bush was a powerful advantage.

Throughout the campaign, Warner would ask friends to go on day trips with him and would call on the spur of the moment for advice or just someone to talk to. Ramsey interrupted a meeting to take a Warner call a week before the election. "He's nervous as a cat," Ramsey reported.

A few days before the election, the fellow Capital Investors were cheering Warner, who was ahead in the polls, but also worried for him. "It's pleasing to see a person who's not a politician run," said Walker. "I hope he doesn't get eaten up when he's in there."

When asked if Walker would ever run for office, he said a quick no. He does not want to monitor what he says to please everyone. "I like to be who I am," he said.

On election eve, group members Ramsey, Fernandez, and Morino gathered around tall tables at the Richmond Marriott's bar, drinking wine and eating chicken wings, crab cakes, and cheeseburgers. They were with Ramsey's wife, Norma, and friends and fellow big-donors Jack Davies, an AOL executive who recently joined Leonsis and Fernandez in Lincoln Holdings, and technology executive Buddy Pickle and his wife, Ginger. Morino, Fernandez, and Davies flew in to Richmond together on a private plane, avoiding the Northern Virginia traffic.

Russ Ramsey especially was in a good mood that night, drinking a cosmopolitan and smoking a cigar. It was about

8 P.M., the polls had been closed for one hour, and Warner was ahead.

The bar television was tuned to the race and Warner's friends looked up from their bites of food and sips of wine every few moments to see the latest percentages from the vote-counting. Ramsey was also getting cell phone updates. "He's exhausted. He hasn't slept in six months," said Ramsey about how Warner was feeling. The lead was not as wide as had been expected. But as it continuously inched toward Warner, Ramsey was informed that a concession telephone call was expected any second from Mark Earley. The group hurried back up to the hotel suite where Warner's family, friends, and big donors were gathered, each wearing an oversize name sign around their neck for security (Fernandez joked that his name tag was worth $100,000). The guys had been there earlier, but escaped to the hotel bar in search of some better wine.

On the way out of the bar, the group was jubilant. Warner is the first Democrat to win the governor's race in Virginia since 1989. But that's not why they're excited. More importantly, Warner is the first of their crowd to win an office of this stature. "We paid for this election," jokes one of them loudly on the way up the elevators.

Up in the private party suite, someone tapped Warner, he walked into the hotel bedroom, soon emerged with an even toothier grin than usual. Cheers arose, glasses were clinked, and cell phone calls were made. Norma Ramsey dialed her Great

Falls home to get her daughter Bailey on the line. Ramsey held up the phone to Madison Warner's ear so the girls could talk about the news. Ramsey said her daughter just wanted to know when she should come for a sleepover in the new house. The Warners are moving to Richmond. The final vote-tallying show Warner at 52 percent and Earley at 47 percent of the votes, with 1 percent for Libertarian candidate William Redpath.

The Warner faithful then surrounded him and moved downstairs en masse in several packed elevators to a staging area behind a grandstand. Many of them, including the Ramseys and Nicholas Perrins and his wife, will stand on a crowded stage with Warner, hitting red, white, and blue balloons up into the air and dancing to what has become the ubiquitous bluegrass music. Warner would almost instantly name Ramsey and Northern Virginia Technology Council president Kilberg to his transition team.

Some of the Warner children's friends were having difficulty getting a ginger ale from the bartender at the cash bar. "This is the difference between Republicans and Democrats," says Fernandez, as he buys tickets for the kids. "We always have an open bar."

The chandelier-filled ballroom was crammed with supporters, most wearing Warner stickers and waving campaign signs. At about 10 P.M., the Earley concession speech was shown on a large screen, followed by much drinking and cheering. About an hour later, Warner and his entourage floated in, taking over the stage to the now-familiar "Warner" song that describes him as "a good ol' boy from up in NoVa-ville."

"Get ready to shout it, from the coal mines to the stills, here comes Mark Warner, the hero of the hills," sang the Bluegrass Brothers.

Warner thanked Mudcat, who wrote the bluegrass campaign song, he thanked his wife, Lisa Collis, and her parents, their children, and numerous others. Warner looked thrilled and stunned. The cheery pop song "Let the Day Begin" by The Call sent an optimistic vibe through the crowd. "Tonight, let's celebrate," shouted Warner. He had just inherited a state with enormous financial, transportation, and tax problems. While only a relative few people would notice if he didn't meet his promises in doing a private venture capital deal, his constituency is now much, much larger. The money-man will also, under a Virginia conflict-of-interest law, have to drastically rearrange his financial life before inauguration day in January, likely putting his investments in a blind trust. For the next four years, Warner won't be concentrating on his own money, but the economy of a region. But finally, he had won. The day he had both fought for and feared is here. But Warner was already thinking about what's next.

"Tomorrow an awful lot of hard work begins."

ACKNOWLEDGMENTS

THIS BOOK COULD NOT have been written without my ability to be a fly on the wall at the dinners or without countless other interviews, phone calls, and email discussions. So first off, thanks to the twenty-six members of the Capital Investors for bearing with me and for sharing their insights, pain, and joy through these past few years. They let me into their world without knowing what I would end up writing, and I am grateful for that. Thanks especially to Jim Kimsey and his friend Joe Robert for calling me the day before a trip to Cartagena, Colombia, and inviting me along to see whatever I might see. And to all the members' schedulers and "chiefs of staff" for setting up interviews, tracking these guys down, and helping me through a few side doors. A tremendous thanks to fund manager Andrew Sachs who ran interference and has a remarkable sense of ease and humor dealing with the group.

Hundreds of interviews make up the background and substance of this book. When I originally set out to write the story of technology in Washington, I had not meant to focus solely on a couple dozen men called the Capital Investors. Many, many more than them deserve credit and blame. Another entire book could be written about the Washingtonians who actually invented the Internet in the first place.

So thanks to all those who rode the technology wave, from the big-dream start-up executives who told me their life stories to the venture capitalist who asked me one day to make sure to tell him about my business "idea" first, he'd invest a few million. Of course, it hit me at that moment how ridiculous it all had become and I feared for his fund. Thanks also to angel investing pioneers John May and Cal Simmons, who didn't mind that I appropriated the name of one of their clubs for the title of this book.

I thank Holidae Hayes, Patty Abramson, and Susan DeFife for not only their dead-on analysis of the group and the individuals, but for showing that technology and finance in Washington is not entirely a boys' club. And I have great appreciation for those entrepreneurs who presented to the group, whether they received investment or not. Thanks for sharing your tale.

Everyone who wants to write a book should be so lucky as to work for *The Washington Post.* Our bosses actually encourage you to do such things and help you along the way. Thank you to our peerless publishers Don Graham and Bo Jones, and to editors Leonard Downie, Steve Coll, and Tom Wilkinson for the time off and advice. Business editor Jill Dutt launched the column I write, and I will always appreciate her willingness to try new things—and the day she took me out for champagne when I got the book deal, when, of course, she was on deadline.

On their own time, Olwen Price transcribed interviews, Mike Stuntz read an early draft, and Bill O'Leary photographed the group, catching the mood of the moment. Photo editor Joe Elbert helped me delve into the archives for the rest of the shots, taken by the talented picture staff of *The Washington Post.*

I began writing about technology in 1995, before, it seemed, most people cared about it. So thank you to the editors who encouraged me to cover the story, including David Ignatius and Andy Jenks, and publishers Andrew Jacobson and John Hurley, who created the magazine *TechCapital* that I had the great experience of editing. Esther Smith gave me my first technology writing job when she convinced me it really wouldn't be that bad working in Tysons Corner, and has been a great mentor ever since. *Congressional Quarterly*'s president and publisher Robert W. Merry encouraged me to write this book and gave me a bit of advice early on that saved at least one big headache.

Thanks to *Washington Post* editors John Burgess, Larry Roberts, Terence O'Hara, Dan Beyers, Tracy Grant, Sandy Sugawara, Nell Henderson, Nancy McKeon, and Pat Sullivan, who make every column and story better. Thanks also to *Post* colleagues Leslie Walker, Fred Barbash, Daniela Deane, Alec Klein, Mark Leibovich, Dina ElBoghdady, Carrie Johnson, Neil Irwin, Kathleen Day, Martha McNeil Hamilton, Warren Brown, Frank Swoboda, Margaret Webb Pressler, Chris Stern, and Amy Joyce who encouraged me to stretch my writing muscles by doing a book, or gave me advice, or just listened. And thanks to the wonderful staff at washingtonpost.com, especially Valerie Voci and Russ Walker.

Acknowledgments

I am enormously thankful to my brilliant literary agent Jan Miller and her colleague Michael Broussard, who make things happen. And to my big-vision editor Dominick Anfuso and his assistant Kristen McGuiness at the Free Press.

I do not belong to a dinner club, but I do have an amazing network of friends and family who supported me along the way: Alison Bermack, Gail Mandel, Alison Meyer, Janina Wetzel, Nick Wakeman, Tania Anderson Harbourt, Kimberly Small, Tim and Sue Reason, Michelle Rysman, Liz Braunstein, George and Elizabeth Kleiber, Beverly and Ron Raphael, Lesley and David Kitts, Sarah Johnstone, and Susan and John Javens. Thanks for reading parts of the manuscript and your continuous, "Are you done yet?"

My parents, Patrick and Dee Henry, have always encouraged by example and great enthusiasm for the choices I've made. If I wanted to accomplish something, they said I could. They were the first readers of this book, of course. Thank you, you are the best.

And most of all, thank you to my number one critic, fan and husband Benjamin Kleiber, who makes me laugh when I need it most and is my partner in all adventures.

Shannon Henry
Cleveland Park
Washington, D.C.
2002

CAPITAL INVESTORS
PORTFOLIO LIST

As of January, 2002

Name of company (investment amount)

CI Portfolio I

Cyveillance ($1,100,000)
KnowledgeMax ($200,000)
Zona Financiera ($1,000,000)*
EqualFooting ($1,230,000)*
Shop2U ($500,000)
FastTide ($400,000)*
Twinbays ($500,000)

CI Portfolio II

MissionFish ($100,000)
WebSurveyor ($300,000)
Cvent.com ($250,000)
Webversa ($250,000)
AweSim ($200,000)*
Opion ($300,000)*
Core Communications ($300,000)
RIVA Commerce ($200,000)
LifeLink MD ($200,000)
Viztec ($200,000)
MaTRICS ($250,000)

*No longer in business

INDEX

Abramson, Patty, 38
Aether Systems, 127, 172
Affleck, Ben, 160
Aggarwal, Reggie, 145–49, 230–33, 237
Akerson, Daniel, 35
Ali, Muhammad, 101
Alliance Bernstein, 133
AmericaWorks, 244
Andersen Consulting, 96
Anderson, John, 159
Andreessen, Marc, xi, 14, 27, 131–32, 154, 181, 216
  and the crash, 102
  influence of, 41–42, 234
  and Loudcloud, 35, 132, 216
  move to Palo Alto, 35–36, 219
  and Netscape, 35, 83, 132
  as public speaker, 57–58
  at social gatherings, 183
Andrews, Ed, 63
angel clubs, nature of, 27, 37–38
angel investors, 2, 11, 38–40, 125
anthrax scares, 215
AOL (America Online), 78–85, 100, 144, 196
  accounting case of, 165
  board of, 36, 263
  and the crash, 9, 135, 201, 206
  early years of, 55, 56, 59
  headquarters of, 67
  influence of, 61, 72, 80–84, 113, 234
  management of, 263
  media ownership by, 80–81
  and 9/11 attacks, 213–14

PAC of, 82
  success of, 71, 263
  Time Warner merger with, 9, 79, 111–15, 131, 197, 214
AOL.com, 77
Ariba, 107
Arnone, Patrick, 58
Ashery, Elie, 63–64
ASM Investments, 105
Associated Communications, 103

Backus, John, 68, 70–71
Baltimore Ravens, 122
Bansal, Sanju, 155, 174, 232
Barbour, Haley, 17, 19, 20
Barksdale, Jim, 67
Barnes, Michael, 258
Barris, Peter, 202
Bennett, Tony, 126
Berkeley, Alfred R. III, xi, 187
  influence of, 31
  at meetings, 41, 45, 46, 47, 48, 49, 52, 219, 221–24, 226–27
  on Nasdaq, 55, 170, 226
Best Buddies Ball (2000), 100–101
Biddle, Jack, 12
Billings, Eric, 117, 255
Bindview Corp., 47
Birchmere Ventures, 146–47, 148
Bisnow, Mark, 159–60, 175, 176
Black Entertainment Television, 35
Bluegrass Brothers, The, 250, 269
Brady Campaign to Prevent Gun Violence, 257–58
Brando, Marlon, 57
"Brat Pack" technology salon, 63

Index

Brookings Institution, The, 57
Buffett, Warren, 119
Bugs Bunny, 112
Bulusu, Suri, 23
Burger King, 113
Burton, John, xi, 36, 51
  investments of, 42–43, 108
  and Legent, 170
  at meetings, 41, 94, 96, 97, 98, 99,
    244, 245
Bush, George W., 21, 264, 265–66
Bushkin, Kathy, 263

Capital Crossover Partners (CCP),
    119–21
Capital Investors:
  author's connection with, 2–5
  beginnings of, 2, 6–7, 26–30, 33,
    38–39, 256
  cast of characters, xi-xiv
  connections of, 29–30, 234–35
  and the crash, 107–14, 125, 229
  and elections, 17–21, 22, 252–53,
    266–68
  follow-on investments avoided
    by, 39–40, 140, 148, 232,
    237–38
  impact of, 14, 28, 72, 77, 162,
    233–35, 246
  individual members of, 11–12,
    199–200; see also specific
    members
  interrelationships within, 8,
    36–37
  meetings of, 3; see also specific
    venues
  mission of, 2, 27, 34, 38–40, 96,
    223–24, 233–38
  and Morino building, 67
  mutual support within, 31–32,
    43, 162, 169, 171, 230, 239,
    252, 255
  new members of, 34–35, 72

and 9/11 attacks, 214–15
  pitching to, 41–43
  portfolio of, 38, 42, 43, 52,
    107–8, 145, 229–39
  as social network, 30–31, 33, 36,
    183–88, 230, 238
  women excluded from, 7, 35, 38
Capital One, 140, 142, 220–21
Capital Rising, 138, 202–4
Caplan, Phil, 77
CapNet, 82
Carlyle Group, The, 232, 244
Carvey, Dana, 151
Case, Jean Villanueva, 263
Case, Steve, ix, 36, 192
  and AOL, 8, 9, 55, 56, 78–82, 84,
    111, 113–15, 197, 198–99,
    201, 234, 263
  influence of, 113, 127, 211, 234
  investments of, 120, 201
  at meetings, 12, 41–42, 235
  and philanthropy, 163
  Ten Commandments of, 81
Casey, Nancy, 169–70, 186, 187
Castro, Fidel, 15–16, 190
Catalyst Solutions, 243–46
Caucus Room, Washington, 73, 106
Caufield, Frank, 36
Celera, 131
Cheney, Richard, 264, 265
CIA (Central Intelligence Agency),
    28
Cidera, 108
Cirque du Soleil, 101
Cisco Systems, 22, 23, 115
Cisneros, Gustavo, 193, 195
Citronelle, Washington, 218–27
Clark, Kathy, 43
Clinton, Bill, 16, 34, 77, 190
Clinton, Chelsea, 75
Clinton, Hillary Rodham, 21
Clooney, George, 160
CNN, 112, 113–14, 196

Cognos, 227
Collis, Lisa, 269
Colombia:
  diplomacy attempts in, 8, 16,
    189–99
  drug trade in, 194
  FARC and, 190, 191, 194, 198
  public image of, 196
Columbia Capital, 50, 142, 253, 255,
  256, 258, 262
Combs, Sean (P. Diddy), 176, 177
Comiskey, Stephen, 133
Compaq, 128–30
CompuServe, 55, 81
Computer Associates, 58
Cooley Godward, 135
Cooter (Ben Jones), 249
Core Capital, 36, 38, 51, 139, 141,
  238
Core Communications, 49–51, 150,
  224
crash, 3–4, 100–112, 115–30
  down rounds in, 125
  dreams lost in, 102, 105, 106
  duration of, 101, 106
  "financing question" in, 104
  layoffs in, 109, 116, 125, 135,
    155, 166, 168, 218, 230, 234
  "liquidity events" in, 229
  margin calls in, 102–3
  market de-listings in, 109
  9/11 attacks and, 214–16
  paper losses in, 103–5, 107–12,
    124
  and post-crash time, 131–35
  profits made in, 105, 117–21, 124
  real estate in, 138, 186
  ripple effect of, 111, 115, 116–17
  stock drops in, 44–45, 101–2,
    104, 115, 124
  survival in, 201
  venture capitalists in, 109–11,
    116, 120, 124–25, 215

vulture capitalists in, 7, 119, 139,
  215
wealth depletion in, 101–2,
  105–6, 108, 200
Cvent, 146–49, 230–32
CyberCash, 29, 36, 124, 137, 140,
  220
CyberMark, 69
Cyveillance, 52, 109

Daniels, Eric, 230
Davies, Jack, 246, 266
Defense Department, U.S., 27
DeFife, Susan, 42–43, 64, 108, 253
Dell, Michael, 21, 30
Democratic National Committee,
  263
Democratic Party of Virginia, 254
Deutsche Bank, 123
DeWitt, Caren, 208
Diana, princess of Wales, 82
Dietz, Jane, 258
Digex, 108, 222
Digital Impact, 215
Dimension Data (DiData), 128–30,
  205, 206, 219
Doceus, Inc., 61
Dole, Bob, 263
"Doonesbury" (cartoon), 159
D'Orta, James, 98, 99, 233
DotTrauma.com, 124
Draper Atlantic, 68, 69, 70
DreamLabs, 264
Dukes of Hazzard, The (TV), 249
Durant, Will and Ariel, 155
Dyson, Esther, 67

Earley, Mark, 243, 248, 251, 253,
  260–62, 264–66, 267–68
Earthlink, 80
eBay, 214, 235
eCiti Cafe, Tysons Corner, 258, 259
"EGO" cards, 50

Ein, Mark, 171
11600 Sunrise Building, 65–71
    and the crash, 125–26
    FastPitch events in, 70–71
    network effect of, 67–68, 70
    Via Cucina in, 68
Ellison, Larry, 21, 170–71
Emtera, 47–48
Entevo, 47
EqualFooting, 52, 263
Everhart, Angie, 101

Fahey, John M., Jr., xi, 111
    at meetings, 46, 48, 94, 95, 96
    and National Geographic, 134
Falk, David, 74
Farrow, Mia, 177
FastPitch, 70–71
FastTide, 142–45
FBR Technology Venture Partners,
    118
Ferguson, Sydney "Nini," 190
Fernandez, Jean-Marie, 126, 129,
    205
Fernandez, Raul, xi, 67, 169, 204–7
    and the crash, 44, 90, 101–2, 103,
        107, 111, 126–31, 136, 214
    early years of, 76
    and elections, 45, 252, 255, 266,
        267, 268
    influence of, 30, 37, 66, 72, 73,
        75–78, 87
    investments of, 127, 133, 206,
        207, 209, 210–11
    "lessons" of, 88
    at meetings, 46, 48, 49, 50, 53, 96,
        98, 107, 245, 246
    and 9/11 attacks, 214
    and Proxicom, 37, 72–73, 77–78,
        87–88, 101–2, 111, 126–30,
        187, 201, 207, 210–11, 213, 219
    public image of, 37, 210
    at social gatherings, 87–88,
        100–101, 124, 126

and sports organizations, 8, 13,
    77, 78, 101, 106–7, 201, 206,
    212–13, 246
Fernandez, Raul (jeweler), 87
Fleet Call, 256
Forbes, 164
Forbes, Steve, 160
Four Seasons, Georgetown, 26
Frederick, Keith, 254–55
Friedman, Billings, Ramsey (FBR)
        Group, 67, 69, 117–18,
        119–20, 164, 232, 255
Friedman, Emanuel "Manny," 117,
    255
Frutkin, Elliott, 61

Gabor, Zsa Zsa, 252
Gates, Bill, 21
Gemplus, 140–41, 142
General Atlantic, 206
General Motors, 72
Georgetown Club, Washington,
    136–50
George Washington University, 30,
    259
Ghose, Suprotik, 22–25
Giannini, David, 49, 224
Gilmore, James S. III, 262
Gingrich, Newt, 249
Giuliani, Rudy, 241
Gladstone, David, 35
Global Internet Ventures, 232
Goldman Sachs, 123, 127, 157, 164
Goldwire, 22
Gorog, William F., xii, 169, 173
    and elections, 260
    and InteliData, 67
    investments of, 37
    and LexisNexis, 11
    at meetings, 47, 94, 96, 99, 219,
        224
    at social gatherings, 124
Graham, Jim, 140–41
Grassroots.com, 258, 263

Grassroots Enterprise, 263
greed, 9, 27, 54, 60, 62
Greenberg, Jerry, 126
Greenfield, Donna, 183, 186, 187
Greenfield, Gary, xii, 93, 253
   and the crash, 137, 138, 201, 216
   at meetings, 47, 48, 51, 137, 138,
      145, 149, 244
   and social gatherings, 87,
      183–88
Greenspan, Alan, 9, 186
GTCR Golder Rauner, 123

Haig, Gen. Alexander, 75, 124, 263
Haig, Wendy, 124
Hanks, Tom, 82
Hart, Christie, 69
Hart, Frederick, 185
Hart, Gary, 263
Harvey, Jamey, 70
Hayes, Holidae, 10, 32, 79, 86, 126,
      132–33, 197–98, 215
Hendrix, Jimi, 172
Hidden Creek Country Club Inn,
      Reston, 26
Holdren, Julie, 168–69
Holtzman, David, 41, 66, 214,
      225–27, 228–29, 236
Hudda, Amir, 47–48
Human Genome Sciences, 30, 131
Humphrey, Doug, 108
Hunt, Helen, 101

ICQ, 81
iKimbo, 70
In-Q-Tel, 28
InteliData, 67
Internet:
   "crash" (2000) of, *see* crash
   "digital divide" of, 87
   heyday of, 10, 12–13, 54–64,
      71–73, 79–87, 89–90, 113–14,
      124, 153, 199
   lawsuits against, 218

   opened to commercial enter-
      prise, 26
   personal wealth created on, 6
   pornography on, 261
ISP Soft, 22

Jackson, Michael, 178
Jagemann, Paula, 72
Jagr, Jaromir, 206, 212
Johnson, Robert, 35
Jonas, Gary, 210
Jones, Ben (Cooter), 249
Jordan, Michael, 8, 13, 73, 74–75,
      77, 106–7, 178, 206, 212–13,
      242, 246
Journey, The (Morino), 58

Karma, 227
Kataria, Anjali, 93–97, 174, 227
Kay, Rick, 246
Kemp, Jack, 72, 76, 252, 263
Kennedy, John F., 255
Kennedy Center for the Arts,
      Washington, 197
Keough, Greg, 61
Khoury, Karl, 258
Kilberg, Bobbie, 264, 268
Kim, Jeong H., xii, 35, 37
   and the crash, 139, 200
   influence of, 28, 76, 234, 246
   investments of, 120, 142, 207,
      231, 232
   and Lucent, 29, 115, 136, 200,
      234
   at meetings, 246
Kimsey, James V., xii, 77, 140, 204
   and AOL, 9, 36, 81, 111, 198–99
   in Colombia, 8, 16, 189–99
   and the crash, 124, 139
   in Cuba, 15–16
   and elections, 255
   influence of, 221, 242
   investments of, 99, 133, 142,
      207

Kimsey, James V. (*continued*)
  at meetings, 18, 19, 23, 24, 25, 95,
    96, 97, 98, 99, 136, 137, 138,
    139, 142, 144, 148–50, 241–42
  and philanthropy, 197
  in post-wealth state, 191, 197
  Saylor encouraged by, 171
  at social gatherings, 10, 183, 198
King, Suzanne, 109–10
Kington, Mark, 255
Kissinger, Henry A., 76
Kmart, 221
KnowledgeMax, 52
Kool and the Gang, 101

Lassus, Marc, 141, 142
Lauder, Estée, 156
Lauren, Ralph, 156
LCC, 173
Ledecky, Jonathan, 246
Lee, Ken, 143–45
Legent Corp., 58, 170
Leonsis, Lynn, 100
Leonsis, Ted, xii
  and AOL, 9, 111, 113–14, 214
  connections of, 37, 72, 73–76, 77,
    120, 171
  and elections, 255, 266
  and Lincoln Holdings, 73–75, 266
  at meetings, 241, 245–46
  public image of, 211–13
  and social gatherings, 100, 126
  and sports organizations, 8,
    73–75, 101, 106, 201, 206,
    212, 213, 242, 246
  "The List" of, 211, 213
"Let the Day Begin," 269
Levine, David, 60–61, 109
Lewis, Tom, 237
LexisNexis, 11
LifeLinkMD, 97–99
Lincoln Holdings, 73–75, 101, 246,
  266

Liz Claiborne, 30
Loudcloud, 35, 102, 132, 216, 232
Lucent Technology, 29, 115, 136,
  200, 234

McClellan, Atlantic, 23–24, 186
Maccoby, Michael, 13
McCurry, Mike, 258, 263
McDonald's, 156
McDonnell, Jack, xiii, 236
  and the crash, 117, 121–24
  and Defense Department, 27
  investments of, 49, 93, 124, 231
  at meetings, 92–94, 95, 97–98,
    221, 223
  and 9/11 attacks, 214, 215
  at social gatherings, 186, 187
  and TNS, 37, 50, 91–92, 121–23,
    184–85, 201
McDonnell, Jackie, 184–85
McDonnell, John J. III, 123–24
McPherson, Mary, 65
MAD magazine, 112
Madonna, 112, 163
Maggiano's, Tysons Corner, 26
Majestic Café, Alexandria, 221
Makihara, Minoru, 193
Mancinelli, Bruce, 233, 236
Mandl, Alex, xii, 24, 38, 187, 204
  and the crash, 103–6, 200–201
  and elections, 252
  influence of, 28, 30
  investments of, 231
  at meetings, 46, 95, 96, 97, 98
  and Teligent, 35, 36, 45, 49,
    103–6, 121, 136, 200, 218
Mandl, Susan, 105
MapQuest, 81
Marks, Art, xii, 12
  connections of, 47, 169–70, 210,
    228
  on the crash, 110, 201–2
  and elections, 252, 255

investments of, 210, 223
at meetings, 45, 50, 51, 52, 223, 224, 241, 242, 245
as money man, 27, 62, 89
at social gatherings, 116, 186, 188
Marulanda, Manuel, 189, 193, 195, 196
Marx, Karl, 20
Mathias, Edward J., xii, 29, 232, 238, 244, 245
MaTRICS, 222–23
May, John, 40
MCI Center, Washington, 73, 206
MCI WorldCom, 59
Meir, Golda, 169
Melton, Bill, xiii, 89, 204, 255
   and AOL, 36, 111
   connections of, 36, 37, 50, 133, 231, 232
   and the crash, 139, 200
   and CyberCash, 29, 36, 124, 137, 140, 220
   investments of, 142, 231, 232
   at meetings, 15, 17, 20, 23, 24, 137, 139, 141–42, 144–45, 147, 148–49, 219, 220, 223, 243
   and VeriFone, 36
Merant, 201
Merrick, Phillip, 176, 208
Merrill Lynch, 214
Michael.com, 151, 153, 178
Microsoft, 112, 204
MicroStrategy:
   board of, 171
   company culture of, 159, 174, 177
   and the crash, 138–39, 151–82
   and Cvent, 232
   departures from, 175–76
   restatements of, 152, 153, 163–65, 168, 169, 174

sales recognition of, 164–65
Saylor and, 8, 18, 31, 72, 100, 136, 151–82, 200
and SEC, 8, 31, 163, 165–66, 168, 180
shareholder lawsuit of, 168, 180
startup and early days of, 154–55, 156–57
stock drop of, 8, 31, 107, 136, 152, 163
and Strategy.com, 157–58, 159, 172–73, 179, 180, 185
Milken, Michael, 162
Milliken, Sean, 234–35
MissionFish, 234–35
Mitsubishi Corporation, 193
Mixer, David, 255
Moody, Jonathan, 153
Moreno, Luis, 192, 196–97
Morino, Mario, xiii, 37, 77
   and CI formation, 26, 28–29
   in Cleveland, 211
   community focus of, 66, 67, 210, 211, 217
   discovery process of, 58–59
   on ego and greed, 54, 60, 62, 163
   and elections, 255, 266
   influence of, 37, 43, 56–57, 59, 64, 65–67, 71, 72, 76, 200, 209
   investments of, 133, 207
   at meetings, 15, 20, 23, 26, 50, 53, 139, 244–45
   memoir of, 58
   philanthropy fund of, 8, 30, 60, 163, 207–10, 217, 239
   and Potomac KnowledgeWay, 55–56, 59, 207
   and Saylor, 169, 170–71
   at social gatherings, 11, 126, 216–17
   vacations of, 64–65
   and World Economic Forum, 199

Morino Associates, 58
Morino building, 65–71, 73, 78,
    125–26, 139, 206, 230
Morino Institute, 57, 59
Morris, Nigel, xiii, 35, 219, 220–21,
    226–27
Morton's, Tysons Corner, 44–53
Moss, Melissa, 89
MRW Enterprises, 262
Murray, James, 255

NASCAR races, 221, 249
Nasdaq, 31, 55, 120, 170, 219, 226,
    227, 231
National Geographic Society, 134
National Institutes of Health, 131
National Rifle Association (NRA),
    257–58
Netpreneur Program, 58, 59–60, 61,
    64, 65, 68, 70, 207–8
Netscape, 35, 81, 82, 83, 132
Network Associates, 203
Network Mantra, 22–25
Network Solutions, 41, 59, 66, 67,
    131, 172, 225
Neuman, Laura, 222–23
New Enterprise Associates (NEA),
    84, 108, 109–10, 116, 201–2,
    215, 223, 228–29
New Jersey Devils, 106, 107
Newsletters.com, 63–64
New York Post, 163
Nextel, 256
Noor, Queen, 198, 241
Northern Virginia Technology
    Council, 264, 268

Olympus Group, 168
1-800-Flowers, 234
onesixtyblue, Washington, 74
123 Club, 33
Opion, 41, 66, 225–27, 228–29
Opryland, 224

Oracle, 170
Oros, Dave, 172
OTG Software, 246

Pacino, Al, 57
Pastrana, Andres, 192–96, 242
Patrick, Dick, 106
Pentagon, Washington, 9/11 attack
    on, 180, 213, 230, 231, 264
People, 160
Perrins, Nicholas, 262, 268
Phillips Collection, 62–63
Pickle, Ginger, 266
Pickle, Kirby "Buddy," 45, 266
Pinson, Marty, 146–49
Pittman, Bob, 79, 81–82, 113, 198
Pittsburgh Penguins, 206
Polaris, 36
Polk, Curtis, 106–7
Pollin, Abe, 73–75, 101
Poretz, Doug, 85
Potomac KnowledgeWay Project,
    55–56, 59, 207
Powell, Colin, 263
presidential election (2000), 17–21, 45
PricewaterhouseCoopers, 163,
    164–65, 167, 180
Prodigy, 55
Proxicom, 100
    board of, 37, 53, 263
    company culture of, 77–78
    competition of, 88
    and the crash, 101–2, 107, 111,
        126–30
    and DiData, 128–30, 187
    growth of, 72–73, 88, 206
    headquarters of, 78, 126
    IPO of, 72, 87, 210–11
    layoffs at, 88, 139
    sale of, 126–30, 187, 201, 207,
        213, 219
    stock drop of, 87, 101–2, 111
    wealth generated by, 72–73, 207

PSINet, 49, 92, 102, 107, 116,
 121–23, 187

Ramsey, Norma, 259, 266, 267–68
Ramsey, Russ, xiii, 28, 77, 89, 161
  and CI formation, 26, 27, 29
  connections of, 47, 59, 73, 117,
   156–57, 164–65, 169, 171, 179
  and the crash, 102, 115, 117–21,
   124, 137–38
  and elections, 255, 258, 259–60,
   266–68
  and FBR, 117–18, 119–20
  hedge fund started by, 7, 30–31,
   99, 120–21, 139, 201, 239
  investments of, 109, 118–21
  at meetings, 15, 17, 20, 21, 23, 24,
   26, 47, 48, 51, 96, 97, 99,
   137–38, 139, 141, 143, 147,
   148, 149, 219, 220, 221, 222,
   224, 226–27, 241, 242–44, 246
  and 9/11 attacks, 215
  at social gatherings, 116, 126,
   258
Razzouk, William, 78–79, 113
Redford, Robert, 177
Redpath, William, 268
Refugees International, 191
Regardie, Bill, 84–86
Regardie, Renay, 85
Regardie's Power, 84–85
Republican Party of Virginia, 254
Restaurant Nora, Washington,
 91–99
Rickertsen, Rick, 117
Ritz-Carlton Hotel, Washington,
 15–25
RIVA Commerce, 93–97, 174
Robert, Joseph, 157, 171, 189–92,
 194, 195
Rosenbaum, Michael, 243–46
Roxio, 219
RPW, 43

Rutt, Jim, 172
Ryan, Meg, 82

Sabre, 215
Sachs, Andrew, 179, 185, 186
  as fund manager, xiv, 26, 30,
   40–41, 52, 53, 93, 150,
   174–75, 224, 235, 238–39
  at meetings, 21, 23, 24, 25, 51, 52,
   95, 97, 140–42, 145, 148–50,
   223, 243, 245–46
Sachs, Heather, 185, 186
"Samurai Six," 123
Sapient, 126
Saunders, Mudcat, 250, 269
Saylor, Michael, xiii
  and the crash, 135, 151–82, 200,
   218
  early years of, 154
  and elections, 255, 258
  house of, 177–78, 186–87, 204
  influence of, 93, 174–75
  at meetings, 18, 19, 20, 21, 23, 24,
   25, 35, 46, 48, 93, 94, 96, 174,
   233
  and MicroStrategy, 8, 18, 31, 72,
   100, 136, 151–82, 200
  and online university, 152, 162,
   210
  personality traits of, 154, 155,
   161, 163, 166, 168–69, 171,
   179, 181–82
  public image of, 37, 158–62,
   168–69, 175, 178–79, 181, 218
  and Sidgmore, 171–73, 179, 185
  at social gatherings, 22, 100–101,
   116, 126, 157, 162, 171,
   176–78, 183, 185, 186–87, 258
  and Strategy.com, 157–58, 159,
   172, 179, 180, 185, 218
  vision of, 158, 159, 162, 180
  working life of, 181–82
Schrader, William, 49, 92, 102, 122

Scott & Stringfellow, 153
SEC (Securities and Exchange
    Commission), 8, 31, 163,
    165–66, 168, 180
September 11 attacks, 180, 213–15,
    230, 231, 240, 241–42, 264–65
Sex.com, 261
Shop2U, 234
Shriver, Sargent and Eunice, 100
Sidgmore, John, xiii, 115, 252
    and the crash, 102, 122, 136, 215
    influence of, 51, 72, 169, 234
    investments of, 99, 120, 207
    at meetings, 41, 45, 46, 47, 49, 50,
        51, 52, 96, 220, 222, 223
    and MicroStrategy, 31
    and Saylor, 171–73, 179, 185
    at social gatherings, 116, 185
    and UUNet, 72, 122, 171
    and WorldCom, 8–9, 234
Silicon Valley envy, 29, 37
Silver, Jonathan, xiii, 34, 89
    and Core Capital, 36, 38, 51, 139,
        141, 238
    and Core Communications, 49,
        224
    at meetings, 21, 45, 51, 98,
        138–45, 147, 149, 214, 222,
        224, 225–26, 243, 244, 246
    as money man, 27, 139
    and 9/11 attacks, 214–15
Simmons, Cal, 40, 260
Singh, Neera, 185
Singh, Rajendra, xiii, 35, 182
    connections of, 32, 36, 121
    on the crash, 105–6
    and LCC, 173
    at meetings, 17, 19, 20–21, 23,
        25, 96–97, 98, 99
    at social gatherings, 185
    on wealth, 14, 105–6, 185
Smith, Esther, 12, 171, 207, 211
Snyder, Dan, 126

SpaceWorks, 256
Spacey, Kevin, 100
Spoon, Alan, xiv
    influence of, 30, 43
    at meetings, 18, 20, 24, 96
    as out-of-town member, 36, 219
Stamas, George, 28, 74, 75, 106–7,
    246
State Department, U.S., 198
Strategy.com, 157–58, 159, 172–73,
    179, 180, 185, 218
SunTrust, 226
SwapDrive, 45–47, 51
Sylvan Learning Systems, 245

Taylor, Elizabeth, 252
Teatro Goldoni, Washington,
    240–46
technology:
    arrogance and, 113, 134, 171,
        178, 199, 261
    competition in, 88
    critical mass of, 56
    "digital divide" of, 87
    guilt of huge success in, 191
    heyday of, 10, 13, 54–64, 71–73,
        79–87, 89–90, 102, 113–14,
        124, 153, 160, 199
    labor supply in, 115–16
    market collapse of, *see* crash
    and philanthropy, 101, 210–11
    power of, 4, 159–60, 267
    public relations in, 161
    social interaction and, 36–37,
        62–63, 100–101, 116, 256
    Washington as a center of, 13,
        21–22, 29, 37, 38, 55–56, 60,
        61, 65–67, 73, 75, 76, 80,
        82–84, 85, 159, 163, 216,
        262–64
Teligent, 24, 35, 36, 45, 49, 103–6,
    121, 136, 200, 215–16, 218
term sheets, 125

terrorism, war on, 216, 242, 264–65
Thayer Capital, 117
Third Edition, Georgetown, 64
Thruport Technologies, 261
Ticketmaster/Citysearch, 73
Time magazine, 112
Time Warner, AOL merger with, 9, 79, 111–15, 131, 197, 214
Tonkel, Jeff, xiv, 29
Torrent Networking Technologies, 257
Transaction Network Services (TNS), 37, 50–51, 91–92, 121–23, 184–85, 201
Travelocity, 215
TravelSmith, 234
Trudeau, Garry, 159
Trusted Information Systems, 203
Turner, Ted, 114

U2, 172
UNext, 162
University of Maryland, 200
University of Virginia (UVA), 31
Unseld, Wes, 74
Updata Capital, 69
US Airways Arena, Washington, 73
US Office Products, 146
UUNet, 59, 72, 122, 131, 171

Valhalla Partners, 202
Varsity Group, 109
venture capitalists, 70
    and the crash, 109–11, 116, 120, 124–25, 215
    goals of, 61–62, 84, 110
    kiss of death for, 228–29
    legacies of, 209–10
    successes of, 63, 257
Venture Philanthropy Partners (VPP), 207–11
VeriFone, 36, 37
VeriSign, 131

Victoria's Secret, 156
Villanueva, Jean (Case), 263
Virginia:
    campaign funding in, 252, 261
    conflict-of-interest law in, 269
    gubernatorial election in, 247–69
    "The Shad" in, 247–51
    turkey hunting in, 249, 258
Virginia Public Access project, 252, 255
Viztec, 140–41, 238–39
Vradenburg, George, 82–83
"vulture funds," 7, 119, 139, 215

Wachovia, 226
Wainger, Liz, 56, 207
Waldack, Bruce, 261
Walker, Steve, xiv, 39, 116, 266
    and the crash, 139, 202
    and Defense Department, 27
    influence of, 203
    investments of, 109, 202–4
    at meetings, 50, 139, 141, 144–45, 147, 150, 241, 243
Walker Ventures, 202
Wall Street Journal, The, 218
Warburg Pincus, 123
Wardell, Keith, 234
Warner, John, 22, 251, 252
Warner, Mark, xiv, 36, 161–62
    and CI formation, 26, 256
    and Columbia Capital, 142, 253, 255, 256, 258, 262
    connections of, 30, 59, 231–32, 253, 255–57, 258, 266
    and the crash, 138, 139
    early years of, 253, 255, 259
    and election, 1, 22, 52, 67, 137, 219, 221–22, 230, 239, 240–41, 242–43, 246, 247–69
    investments of, 43, 95, 97, 99, 108, 120, 133, 142, 207, 209–10, 221, 253, 256

Warner, Mark (*continued*)
  at meetings, 26, 33, 46, 47, 48, 49,
    50, 51, 93, 94, 95–97, 99, 138,
    139, 142, 146, 219, 220
  personality traits of, 253–54, 260
  public image of, 254, 260
  at social gatherings, 116, 230,
    258–59
Warner Bros., 112, 246
Washington, D.C.:
  as economic center, 27–28
  knowledge economy base in, 59
  life sciences industry in, 131
  Morino Building in, 65–71
  National Airport, 264–65
  new rich of, 37
  9/11 attacks on, 180, 213
  philanthropy in, 208
  political arena of, 21–22, 27–28,
    37, 66, 76, 262–64
  pretentiousness in, 211
  relationships shaped by, 28–29
  sports organizations in, 73–75, 212
  as tech center, 13, 21–22, 29, 37,
    38, 55–56, 60, 61, 65–67, 73,
    75, 76, 80, 82–84, 85, 159,
    163, 216, 262–64
  venture capital in, 61–62, 63, 84
Washington Business Journal, 162, 210
Washington Capitals, 73, 75, 78,
    106, 107, 212, 246
Washington Mystics, 73
Washington Opera, 197
Washington Post, The, 36, 43, 116,
    153, 160, 178, 265

Washington Power, 133
Washington Sports, 75
Washington Wizards, 8, 73, 74, 107,
    212–13, 246
wealth:
  as the American dream, 253
  creation of, 6
  effects of, 86–87, 134
  high-tech, 73
  and philanthropy, 86–87
webMethods, 118, 144, 176, 208
WebSurveyer, 233
Webversa, 150, 237
Wilder, Douglas, 254
Witzel, Fran, 68, 70
Wolf, Stephen, 192
WomenAngels.net, 38
WomenCONNECT.com, 42–43, 64,
    108
Women's Consumer Network, 89
WorldCom, 8–9, 31, 59, 71, 102,
    131, 171, 234
World Economic Forum, 199
World Trade Center, 9/11 attacks
    on, 180, 213–14, 241–42, 264

XM Satellite Radio, 257

Yahoo, 153, 176, 205, 226
Young, April, 135
You've Got Mail (film), 82
Yurie Systems, 115, 200

Zarpas, Steve, 63
Zona Financiera, 230, 257